POETRY

from Private and Public Places

First published by Botsotso in 2018

Box 30952
Braamfontein
2017

Email: botsotso@artslink.co.za
Website: www.botsotso.org.za

ISBN: 978-0-9947081-2-0

Editors:
Allan Kolski Horwitz, Siphiwe ka Ngwenya, Mboneni Ike Muila

Design, layout and make-up
Vivienne Preston

Botsotso would like to thank the National Arts Council of South Africa
for supporting the publication of this collection.

NATIONAL ARTS COUNCIL
OF SOUTH AFRICA

an agency of the
Department of Arts and Culture

Editorial

With over seventy poets represented, this is a bumper edition of the journal and given the number of interesting and accomplished poems received (over the past two years since publication of Botsotso 17), we believed it worthwhile to break from tradition and dedicate this edition wholly to poetry. However, in addition, an equivalent volume of short fiction and essays will soon be published as the number of powerful stories that reached us was similarly impressive.

In general, the last two years have been very difficult ones for southern Africa. Between Zuma, Mugabe, Mswati and the Mozambican and Lesotho elites, new heights of corruption, megalomania and abuse of state power meant that millions of people continued to languish in poverty and were subject to extreme exploitation by equally corrupt Big Business classes. Fortunately Mugabe and Zuma are themselves becoming features of the past but their legacies of shame will live on for some time – particularly if their highly compromised and decadent parties continue to rule.

What has this political and economic deadlock meant for the arts? How have art-makers (in all the different forms) responded to this historic and tragic setback for liberation from colonialism and apartheid?

Knowing that it was always going to be a struggle to shift the consciousness of the generations of whites tainted by racism and the right to exploit, artists ought to be in the forefront of exposing the notion that Africanization of our society would automatically entail the corruption and mismanagement that Fanon and others foresaw for the post-liberation epoch. That southern Africa has not escaped this depressing situation – and seen a corresponding surge in capitalist (both white and black) accumulation/concentration –

certainly gives us 'food for thought'. Artists need to 'talk back' to all abuses of power -black or white, local or global – so that our critique is honest and as objective as possible: shielding any party from criticism is self-defeating for the whole of society but especially for the black majority who are so marginalised and in need of drastic change in order to access the means for living decent lives.

But what has been the 'artist' response (and more specifically the writers, poets and theatre-makers)? While a recent study of grade 4 South African children has shown that over 80% do not understand what they read, that the state and school library systems continue to ignore the work of local writers, that book chains have converted to an exclusive system of 'sale or return' driving publishers and distributors out of business, we still lack a writers or performing arts organization that can take up issues, both specific to art production and to the more general matters of cultural diversity, language use and development, the media and communication, as well as literacy. And, as such, we have no organised way to respond to the continuing stagnation of vernacular languages, low levels of interest in southern African creative writing and widespread functional illiteracy.

In general, despite the need for exploring/analyzing/commenting on this tragic neo-colonial betrayal, the arts step clear and leave the consciousness and aspirational values of the working class to be shaped by the predictable routines of television soap opera, music that is largely vacuous Afro-pop/gospel/hip-hop, game shows and celebrity spotlights. Of course, the failure of the SABC to raise our general awareness of South Africa's position in Africa, other inter-African contacts and the wider world is a serious obstacle to political development. And this failure to properly 'inform and educate' and to instead entertain at the most basic level, is a good indicator of how the 'transformation' process has largely been squandered for individual short term financial gain through networks of patronage.

And so, given all these critical breakdowns, we are in a period of depression and uncertainty, desperately needing new movements and fresh leadership in all spheres of society. (It is telling that even the very necessary "Fees must Fall/Rhodes must Fall" student movements seem to have collapsed into sectarian and nationalist divisions.)

But is this the whole picture? Fortunately not. For this selection of poems shows that many artists are still sensitively engaging with the issues that affect us as social beings as well as those more private aspects of our complex lives. And is this not the true expression of Ubuntu and the 'I-Thou' relationship in which the 'I' recognises the 'Other' as an equal and as 'worthy of consideration' as itself?

As such, despite the gloom, Botsotso will attempt to provide a platform for work that is relevant, well crafted and beyond cliché.

Contents

Special feature

Sodom and Gomorrah

1 *Napo Masheane*

No 53, Fourth Avenue, Sodom Road, Gomorrah
Rats out-number newborns
Block all sanitation
Cockroach flowing gutters
Flies never go on strike
One cannot get out of ghetto skin colour
Here poverty is a silent sob
Hanging like a coat
Only three minutes from homelessness
Your feeble hands cannot hold a spoon
A good dinner is *papa le metsi a letswai*
Inside a six pile garbage dump
The only dividing thing
Between them and us is the Dead Sea
Sandton City's crystal mirrors glow to your face
Hours romancing your life like a painting
On their walls your wounds are forever bleeding
Even when you can smell the sweet baked cake
On the other side
Waking up
Surrounded by weed
Nyaope man swigged an axe on another
Chicken blood splattered
Where only yesterday children played
Mathini, mogusha, morabaraba le ma-dice
Two hours later sirens are heard
Slow motion police drive through dark alleys
Young girl stabbed by a kiss
Mother screams tear through the sky
Tears gather tears
How does one dream a way out?
How does one dream through the night?

Miscegenation

2 *M.Labuschagne*

"What possessed you to marry the black woman?" scolded his sister.

His older brother also jumped in: "Do you really want your
children to be half-breeds?
Our father would have turned in his grave if he should know!"

"Look", said his sister and pushed her finger in his face, "either you leave her
or we want nothing to do with you anymore!"

Anguished, he went into the veld to meditate and pray.

The next day Miriam and Aaron's skins were whitened with
leprosy.

Moses had to think: *His sense for irony is always flawless.*

You Flew the Calculus of the World

3 *Awogbemila Temitope Ayodeji*

Axiom i: ∫dy/dx. : where x is the a winged   world of Integrable derivatives - I,   you, two mp3
players and Mobutu * Four of us were shadows   of ourselves, the world breaths in
multiples of four.

Axiom ii: Our shadows flew into   a trance of lost reverie -   yours and
mine

Because you mistakenly punched   the sun twice   and un-fattened into two
stars,   four of us walked to discover   our shadows sick of this
unwise followership from the crack   of
dawn.

In its wake, you tripped the light   fantastic into axiom ii   and thudded twice, twice, Not!
You are brave and kindly!

Axiom iii: Avoid Crucifixion at a cost. Your mp3 player paused itself   when boogies couldn't make
us kerfs ,   It's your calculous body of   humanitarian service.

Out of the blue! In your pouch,   an android's Mp3 player's   screen touched itself,

Played itself,   got us unfocused in a way   that focused
us,

It played a soul-Asylum's track   *– runaway train*   and got its sound sway
ready to play Michael Jackson's   *– we are the world.*   It opinioned
us to wave ourselves wrinkled   into the mouth of a waifish
orphan,

 His profile intertwined with   advanced level poverty etched   on his forehead: "Scampered
while vaulting back to Mongono,   *with crutches to*   *discover his missing leg,*
lost"

He opened his mouth, we found   you, He opened it further to   holler "help", Plus we found
Mobutu obscuring in his cry,   He opened it in details, Am lost,   Unfound flying down his throat,
Only you was sitting   on his tongue, yapping. You   wore skin-made dark mask

With a bad buzz sore and a small   slice of sorrow sewn sedulously,   For lack of battle, For we

were three darker hound's-tooth   motifs, Un-bedazzled.   Then, the
you outside heard   the song skipping in axiom iii   Chanting
through   The second song, whose song sung was a sign of the world's
calculus, am brought into being!

The world chanted you, us -   Suited up with a waif's mouth,
A frail, petite waif
yet   to eat today, Help! The sun   is here to
launch her revenge,   the sun stays as a star.

     You feed him – you've fed yourself.   You saved the world
inside a waif
     You unknotted the *calculus of the world.*   *You flew axiom four. Where*
y is you,

$$\int \int\int\int_{me} Kindness \; ^{dy}\!/_{d(world)} \; d(Mobutu) = humanitar\text{-}$$
ian services.

*Mobutu: any other person that doesn't want to be me or you.

4 *Three poems by NATALIE RAILOUN*

Poised Poems

they come to me when I am alone
driving
walking

places where another's sound is pushed out by
the rush of wind or drone of an engine
spat away by the ocean spume
rustled out by south-easter leaves

clearing a space to make my own noise

Slinky

black cat, emerald eyes
small bandy legs stride steady
even debonair
bringing me your shrew gift
a devoted rub against my ankle
a cat wink smile

Bona fide

sunrise and sunset emerge the same
from the mouth of the shadow spectre

reality could be a hallucination
or worse

a
lie

*

naked in free fall
swindled, out of sparkles

but all light is one light
any warmth a savior
every hand gracious
every breath indebted

to the clouds in free verse
to the creature in free form

❺ *Three poems by MIKE ALFRED*

Now I can tell you …

I can tell you that our marriage
was one of your great creations,
a complete existence but so silent
and modest, I seldom noticed.

I can tell you that our marriage,
such a splendid journey, provided
a way of being, an enchanted life,
a completeness now so fractured.

Diversion:
I wonder where Maslow slotted
a good marriage into his hierarchy
of human seeking? After all, it's one
of life's greatest challenges; something
to be placed at the apex of achievement.
Perhaps he didn't think it as important
as making money or being President.
Good Housekeeping doesn't list
the Top Hundred Marriages.

I can tell you that you bequeathed
me a solidity. You ushered me, callow
youth, into an adulthood where
I function with care, restraint and
learnings from your laughter and
your generous human wisdom.

Tea and cake

Two fading business friends, meet
now and then, over coffee and cake.
They no longer talk business which
has lost all fascination. Their talk
involves reading and writing, a life
ignored. One day, they both confess
that they really wanted to be Ernest
Hemingway; one for the fame, one
for the lifestyle. Neither considered
the writing: the blocks, the blanks, the
black despair, the critics, merciless. But
then they acknowledge the shotgun, that
hopeless end, and return to tea and cake.

As in: he was a man who had to have a woman.

So you're the woman he had to have?
[The extra room is built and furnished.]
Did you allow him to have to have you?
[The grass is beginning to grow again.]
Are you the sort, a man who has to have
a woman, has to have? He was there and
you, you were there. There was music
and dancing, so you danced, and you hardly
invented talking, but you used it well, and
walking, too. [The double bed is soft and warm.]
Yes, he's a man who needs a woman. You're
not the sort who has to have a man, beyond
a need to be needed. Was it Kismet, you were
there and he was there. You, stirring an adoration
he can't fully explain; you, with the gorgeous
eyes, you, the figure among the trees and the
clay vessels. You, the woman who sold her
flat and transferred the cutlery. He was
a man who needed a woman and you,
could you have been anyone else, any
other longing, any other neediness?

6 *Two poems by THOKOZILE MADONKO*

Everything breaks against the mountain

I

Everything breaks against the mountain
The light
The wind

A small part crumbles and shifts against a shattering
The light will not be the same and it will move
And the breeze has shifted bringing a new scent.

The mountain does not stay the same
Everything breaks it
It was closer to the ocean
Did it retreat in fear of the change
The mountain made
As it broke against it?

II

Finding my people.
Sharing a poem
A mourning
I cry when I hear a poem read
Tears as much about the poem as
The poet

There is a longing for their pen,
Their skin
To write to sign the words and rhymes

III

There is a saltiness in the air
A shadow cast by rock and stone
The air dry and the lonely revelation
Of the solitary pen
That breaks against the mountain.

Stellenbosch

In an old ladies house
The smell hits
There is death here
Below these mountains
Small grapes (vine) away the real truth here
This land
Water turned to wine
Very few spared except those allowed a dop or two
To keep the weekends short and sleep

The old ones will say something
A whispering of blood on hands and feet

Unveil the mountain draw back
The curtain
Let their deaths find meaning.

Kula Kokwana

Ti dya ti ya endzhutini ka kokwana
Xikomu se xa hlomuka embhinyini
Ndima yona, u boxile
Mihandzu ya ntamu wa kwe ndzi dyile

U ndzi wundlile kokwana
U ndzi kombile rirhandzu swonghasi
U wile a pfuka na mina
A ndzi ongola loko ndzi vabya

A ndzi bebula hi ndzhovo,
A ndzi mbuwetela loko ndzi rila
A ndzi swekela switsongo
A ndzi kufumeta hi vuxika

Namunthla ndzi kurile kaa!
U ndzi kurisile hi rirhandzu mukhegula loyi
Ndza swi kota ku yima ndzi tihandzela,
Xi ndzi dyondzisile xikoxa lexi

Ndzi ba mandla ndzi vuyelela,
Ndzi khensa rirhandzu ra ku kokwana
A ndzi tava mani loko a wulo ndzi hlamba mandla?
Milawu a ndzi ta dyondzisa hi mani?

Xipiring!!!!

Xo ghi! ghi! ghi!
Senge kubiwa mancomani cxifuveni
Nyuku ndzururururu!!!
Senge ndzilo wela hi mberha
Hi luya wa hundza
Fambelo ra kona, xiswi tongela bya sekwa
Se i masiku ndzin'wi veke tihlo
Loko a humelela ndza n'oka
Tshumba rivupfile,
Boxa Munwanati, do!!!
Nomo damarheli
Ripfalo vuyavuyani
Halahala, halahala senge ndzi lahle zukwa,
Ndzinga lahlanga nchumu
Loko ndzo kelu ndzin'wi vona arikuteni hile mpfhukeni,
Ndzi cinca na ndlela
Loko o phalakaxa kwala ndzinga kona,
Mbilu yaba senge yingo phohla xifuveni
Swandla swi sungula kujuluka,
Matsolo ya gundla gundla bya xihloka xa khale
Loko ndzi pfula nomo,
Ndzi tela hi manghanghamele
Ntombhi hundzi!!
Na nyamunthla switsandzile

Indonesia

The bending road along the jungle of whispering bamboo
The narrow asphalted road along tall teak and abaca trees
The road of roaring trucks coming down the hill
Green trucks full of logs or quarried stone or scooters
Noses edging close to the cliff
Where wreckage and skeletons sprawl
The heavy silent, grieving forests and caves
      Oh, Indonesia, Indonesia
    I get drunk on your toxic beauty

The road zigzagging through green rice patches and cocoa beans
Large fields of sugar cane, banana and coconut
Large fields of cashew nuts, pineapple and pepper
Fields of tobacco and sweet hairy rambutan
The bashful rain always kisses the ground
But I wonder who owns the seeds and harvest of your sweat
For your children, Indonesia, drill holes in their lungs
With Sampoerma cigarette blades to bury smells of poverty
      Indonesia, Indonesia
    I get drunk on your deadly beauty

Youth climb on the blaring Honda and Suzuki motorbikes
Bravely mingle between roaring trucks and buses
A farmer proudly carries bunch of green banana fruit on his bike
A farmer proudly carries a bunch of green bananas on his bike
Another carries loads of coconut and sells by the roadside
Another carries bamboo leaves to feed his sheep
Before he retires to his crowded home
      Indonesia, Indonesia
    I get drunk on your deadly beauty

Earthquakes, landslides and tsunamis wash away
Burning lakes and dissolving mountains that spit fire
Somehow people have not lost their smile
They patch themselves on the highlands
Knowledge passed to them by their ancestors and oral poets
     Indonesia, Indonesia
   I get drunk on your deadly beauty

The road along brown murky canals of garbage
The road along cruel bitter rivers of dead fish
The whistling winds of Java sea full of oil-drunken gliding dying swans
At the break of dawn, village children swim in rivers and catch typhoid
Mothers wash and hang their sorrows of unemployment on the banks
Men catch trout, maintain sticky silence as their slim and small daughters
Entertain tourists in the brothels of Bali and Jakarta
    Oh, Indonesia, Indonesia
   I get drunk on your deadly beauty

Burgersfort Landfill

Vultures dwell here
Among the grim faced shack dwellers
With their famished children

When the waste delivery truck arrives
The dark human vultures shove and shuffle
Fighting over dirt
Competing with rats and pigs

No one talks about this grim enterprise
The vultures hope to turn rags to riches
In this, our wasted market economy

When ministers talk of black empowerment
No one mentions this grim enterprise
Which tries in vain to turn rags to riches

But on election day –
The vultures are fed with pap and beef stew
Dressed in a clean T-shirt with the leader's face

And when darkness falls
The vultures jadedly retire to the dump
A celestial graveyard of hopes – their home

9 *Two poems by SANET VAN RENSBURG*

Lunch with the Pied Piper

From across the table I examine your eyes
puffy from sleeping in the sun

you're older than I remember
        forearms crossed   twitching like last time
you're softer
as a melody escapes your mouth
and angst sweat pounds from my pores

I follow you revisiting alleys we have explored
and those we avoided before:
Mojitos.
Chivas.
Marlboro.
and us

molten   I submit to your gaze
the diamond flashes when you grab my hand
our knees touch as you say:
'It's an unusual cut. Did you choose it together?'

arrested:
mesmerized and flushed I watch you eat
talking rampantly against the tides of blood
now thrashing through my head
and as a mere conquest
quivering before you
I wonder just why
our embrace
fits so perfectly

Wasted

My bangles flash for you
they shimmer
lashes long and dressed for you
and tears fall
as you savour hers

theirs   even

The boy I kissed at the Greenhouse

1 0 *Gabriel Hoosain Khan*

The tender aloe is aflame, veld fire at night.
Across a hilltop, ever moving, a line of light
On a moonless night.

It starts with a scurrying sound.
The rodents are moving,
I feel them around my feet.

That sweet smell, of burnt dry leaves, grass and trees,
A revolution, in plumes of swirling black smoke.
The smell of singed flesh and fur.

I kissed him against the gate of the greenhouse.
We were alone, his lips pink, his mouth
An open and inviting chasm.

The veld fire across the hilltop
At night time, a smooth curved line of light,
In the distance, ever encroaching,

Eating life, turning it into soot. The smoke now
Unseen, at first gives me a sultry, gentle choke,
And then with violence, our camp is surrounded.

Another boy, I, too, kissed, against the wall
Of an abandoned farmhouse. The house is now in flames.
We were young, he started this fire.

The Wave

❶❶ *Dorothy Murray*

What is this wave which breaks upon the shore
Of my ageing mind washing it so clear
That nothing remains, no single line or mark
To prove that a second past a thought was there
A name, a person now forgotten, swept
Backwards by the tide into a vast ocean
Where it is tumbled until that certain force
Drives it forward once more upon the beach
Where I walk slowly filled with inward fear
That what my memory's lost I may not see
Before the next wave, surging forward
Obliterates all in its driving thrust –
Yet still I stoop, hoping on that sand to find
A shell of thought, a wrack of my own mind.

Colibri for a girl

1 2 *Lepota Cosmo*

Indigo and silk
Gentle breeze
Feathers torn
Among the paper flowers
Twigs and kestrel
Light plays chess
On your eyelashes
The child chooses
Between swords and hummingbirds
The girl blonde
The child chooses
Between sabres and pirates
Golden girl
While the piano plays
Tintin

Promise

In January 1980, I stood knocking on the door of 100 Tugela Way, Portland, Mitchells Plain. It was a Monday morning and I was there to leave a message from my friend Willie.
While I waited I secured my size-28, postman's bicycle with a chain to the tar-pole of the car-port of the house. Meanwhile my knock had been answered and I eventually became aware of this presence straight out the Songs of Solomon: "She was dark and comely". And she was laughing at me.
I discovered later when were dating that she was laughing at me and this bike of antiquity. She was also amused by my old balie fisherman's' haversack which was full of emptiness except for a diary, an apple and a small, hard-covered collection of John Milton's poetry. Sometime in the course of that year I wrote her this poem ...

                    in
                    the
                withering
                    of
                    a
                    leaf
                    in
    the

                                        fading
                    of
    the

                                    day
                    i
                love
                you

(The poem was accompanied by a leaf as green as our young love).

So Much to Declare

During a visit to the USA in May 2013 I found a way to calm my
spirit as I stood in line for the intimidating ways of 'Homeland
Security'. I would play on my i-pod Chris McGregor's 'Country
Cooking' to remind myself that God loves me and the hostile dude
in uniform without measure.
Entering Mzansi in 1982 after a visit to the UK, I had poetry as my
rock and shield.

London, a frozen, dark distance
from sunny skies over Joburg
as BA flight 307 touches ground
on my anxious land. Yet rejoice, O my soul.

AJ Luthuli International Airport
where the open doors
of peace and friendship welcome all
who love freedom and our people
to a liberated South Africa.

Blue eyes,
warm beneath
the peaked cap of officialdom,
admires the miniature bust of VI Lenin,
COLLETS price tag still intact.

Porters on lunch-time break
grin amandla smiles.
Mbaqanga happiness
forms the excited queue.
I wonder how the debate about a new name for our country was
faring and Phila's suggestion that the Settlers Monument in Rhini,
once Grahamstown, be made into the biggest beer-hall in the
Eastern Cape.

And last year, like a dream, walking with Fidel Castro along
Bernard Fortuin Avenue pass the Alex la Guma Cultural Centre

in Elsies River where the Orient Bioscope used to be, and the
Commandante laughing through his beard at my account of how
we youngsters used to cheer when Zorro rode onto the screen
and into our lives. And Daniel, (yes, man, Daniel Ortega) saying
that they did the same when he was a boy in Managua and Che
somewhere in jungled Bolivia.

"Anything to declare?"
Voice hard
blue eyes hard
like rock
tumbling down,
crashing ten-storeys down,
dangling like time.

"Anything to declare?"
Blue eyes shouting,
"Ja, Boesman, with your wing-tip shoes,
button-down collar and new blue suit.
This is South Africa!"
Anything to declare?"
whipping up the Riotous Assembly of my fear.

"Yes," I smile from the tip of my trembling toes,
"South Africa belongs to all, and to me and you, Piet."
He does not hear the roar of 'Mayibuye!' at Freedom Square.
"The People Shall Govern," I assure him,
speaking now with the voice of the thousands
who gathered at The Congress of the People.
"Goed. You may go."

I pick up my suitcase
and my ruffled courage and walk
past security,
past the soldiers.
My Mandela T-shirt,
sweat-wet
against my beating heart . . .

When the hills were dark
For Mzi Mbangula: rest in peace, comrade of my youth.

During 1981 I attended a YCS conference in SOWETO. On the way back, Zelda Holtzman who I met in Joburg suggested that we visit the mother of a friend in Zweletemba on our way through Worcester. The friend in question was Mzi Mbangula, the nephew of Rev Otto Mbangula. I had known Mzi and he and Simon Fredericks were both YCS activists and had gone into exile at more or less the same time. Mzi was an astute observer with a keen intellect, complemented by his wry wit and easy laugh. When we met Ma Mbangula, her opening question to Zelda was "Where is my child?" That moment unlocked the following poem

On a morning such as this.
when the hills were dark
        with the colour
          of burnt dark.
And the sun in the wind
was soft upon
      the land.
And the streets of the places
where we live
     were very still.
On a morning such as this.
when the hills were dark
      when not even your mother knew
you left us.

Poetic Script

1 4 *BOTSOTSO JESTERS*

Ike	I am skinny bowler wind skeleton touch spoko mathambo by virtue of birth I can read the scareness in your eyes
Allan	mps travel in 4x4 style corporates build a massive share option and bonus pile while in the ghetto, unemployed kids become suicide projectiles
Siphiwe	I have an urge like burning fire let me release this flood of desire on every woman I meet before I spit
Ike	bully bull brand beef stalk in your face prima facie redtape windhoek hushpuppy doll check it rubber neck bell ringing moo more school in
Allan	Affirmative Action with a touch of class line up for directorships and down a full glass and if there's trouble Juju and Jimmy Manyi will cover my arse
Siphiwe	I am a hawker in a jozi street cops stole the fish on my dish but haai! I have not lost my jester speech
Ike	to my health supervisor ringas before suffer gate mummy blue skatie pass the dice deal with the root of poor health poverty
Allan	I am the man with the randlord tan don't pull at my skin or scratch 'cause underneath the gold is an umlungu whose met his match
Siphiwe	I raise a Diepsloot fire because of rumour from MaMgobhozi's bitter sense of humour poking the government's expanding brain tumour
All	Botsotso Jesters!

Somewhere

Somewhere
inside a block of flats
a trombone wields a blue flame
then dies

Somewhere
in the wake of surburban silence
a cigarette cough ruptures a lung
then quietly sleeps

Somewhere
inside our tyrant
black screams rise from a burning tyre
refusing to deny

Somewhere
across a treacherous road
a racist hound grinds her teeth
unashamedly

Somewhere
behind a curtained window
a candle sobs
slowly suffocates

Somewhere
beneath the crack of mooonshine
rust permeates dawn
tarnishing our silver dreams

Somewhere
behind shut doors and the electric strings
of wired fences
I roam and return darkly

Saxturns

Sax-junky
when last did you bath?
prrrhhh!!!
your farting blow
chops and changes
a fatal silence
releases a new complexion

You laugh where I dance
when last did you bath?
hei...hei...heee...tuu!
burning sensation
let me out
hei...hei...heee...tuu!
stinky sax blowing
ins and out
in and out
when last did you brush your mouth?

Dear-dee-dirty-sax
strokin a dragon's breath
tongue tasting granadillas
your blow head-rushes-blood-shot-eyes
sting of fire rising
last drag of dying pipe skyf
romantic dragon
wild and extreme
within inner-glows
of your trumpet blows
I burn

pleeeaz
let me out..!

Tshidi's Lobola
(Cousin Tshidi's Lobola kitchen party in Killarney - not Parktown but Orlando West, trackside of Phomolong near Ndofire)

Yes yes y'all

Whiskey dream
a thousand Naigas
in Soweto
me firing

Reprimanding
dancing
hind legs kissing the skies

Bassline
chanting
rebel/ions
soul sisters
showing love

Festive flame licking slowly
the generator of the soul
I am still in recovery mode
how are you ?

Tlou's blues

I shred
against your tearing light
endlessly
gently worming out of the cracks
finding moist more than often
and the glint of feathered dreams
boisterous rainbow
blistering golden beyond the sunset

Malakabe

lerato lena ke mollo
mosi wa lona ha o hloke
patsi le disu hore o kunkele
o thunya ka pelong

ha ke batle ho bua ka malakabe
mashala a lona ke a tshaba
ke nna ona ke molora
le ntjele la nqeta

Sebankanyana le Motsotso

tshupa nako ha e na motsotsonyana
ofetang dihora ka monyaka empa nna le wena
ha re ka o fumana motsotso
metsotswana e tla tswala
thabo le nyakallo
ya pale ya lerato
e tla phelang ka ho sa feleng
ditshomong le dipineng
tse tla binwang ho isa
molokong wa ho qetela

Ha Ke o Hopola

Mahlo a ka a tlala bofufu
Le kutlo ha ke sa na yona
Ho sasanka wena feela
Ka pelong ena e dumang
Ho dumaela wena feela
Ka hloohong ena e sa nkeng hantle

Ha Pelo Nkise

ka molomo ke sitwa
ho hlalosa tsela
tse mashome a mane
le mekgwa e menahaneng
eo ke lakatsang ho e sebedisa
ho tla ho wena botebong
ke tla butle ke tsamaya
le morethetho wa mofehelo wa hao
ke akofile ke fokalla
le sekgahla sa mohoo wa hao
matsoho aka a o matha hohle
leoto la hao le ile marulelong
le leng le sa itsebe le ho kae
aka ona ke sa utlwa hore
a matha thoteng di feng
ho phallang ele madi
maikutlo a ile ha pelo
ntshupise tsela, mmele o se o ile

*

mosuwe o nthutile bophelo
ka morethetho le dikapolelo
a nthuta hore lentswe
ke le bope jwang
noto ebe e feng
ha ke bina "hlooho, mahetla sefuba le letheka.."
empa wena o mosuwe hlooho
o nthutile melodi le methallere
noto ebe e feng
ha se ke tshetse
ka nqane ho puo
ke bina mmele, pelo lo moya
mangole ke se ke a tlotse

Cobus

i was always in one piece
til i was 15 years old

small, so small you said
and i was

you always understood things
the opposite way

'you see that, that's the world'

you tried your best
to turn it around for me
but i wasn't interested –
i cared only for what i had found:

the fine-drawn lines
round your eyes
and how they grew deeper
when i cried;

the way i shook
beneath your strength.

i was always
tearing the skin off things
and your patience
finally grew too tired to hold.

your words
now stamp their anger out
all over me

and i shrink back
my mind cracked
like an egg
on the rim of a bowl.

but i still dream of your sun-filtered curtains
fluttering across my face,
of watching their patterns on the wall . . .

i want to know something else.

adam, by eve

pitted cheek,
igneous rock
whittled even by sobriety and a blade

shoulders,
freed from the heaviness of breast,
supporting unbuckled breadth

nipples lying low
with the shame of redundancy

callous fingertips
on masterful hands

muscles that bunch and loosen
as the mechanisms of masculine movement
run sturdy and smooth

fissures of skin,
folds of aged wood
commanded outwards by touch,
inwards by neglect

from eve –
madonna, whore, virgin

eve, watching.

Unconscious conscience

I take it ill that I misunderstood
Laughed childishly
Cried silently
Questioned unconsciously
Smiled generously
Shared kindly
I took pleasure in being trapped
Hopeless
Crippled.

Was it all an awakening of the neglected conscience?

Remind me

The cheap wine stains
Red lipstick remains
Weave strands
A few rands.

I forgot your name
Your funny English name
I remember your bright brown eyes
Eyes that tell no lies.

Why do you live in a suitcase?
Why do you pack all of your emotions?
It is worn out – your face
It's showing all your commotions.

Gorgeous girl
Graceful girl
Smart girl
Hurting girl.

A Meditation on Certain Times and Places
(Celebrating the life of Gerald Kraak at his wake*)

1 **9** *Stephen Faulkner*

Joburg –
The cold facts first.
Cancer
Spreading
Creeping into secret crevices
Closing down organs
Snatching breath
Almost stealing hope
Almost
Too soon
Too soon
Then the slipping slipping
Quietly away..........

Amsterdam –
I am not fighting for 'them'
I refuse to be part of the problem
How I miss you all
I will not twiddle my thumbs
We must build our own anti-army
Of resistors
How I miss you all
The politics on the outside
Almost as scary
As the politics on the inside
How I miss you all
I will not be settled
I am not resident
Please visit when you can
How I miss you all
How I miss you all

London –
It's nice out.
Those long night strolls
Through Highbury Fields and Finsbury Park
To the pub
The fickle English
Their living caricatures
Of Cor Blimey and Watcha Mate!

Archway North London –
The claustrophobia of exile politics
Relieved only by countless movies
And an abundance of live music
An occasional glass of vino
And a whiskey
Or Two…..
Four, Six, Eight
Motorway with the Tom Robinson Band
Jo Strummer's London Calling
Coming to life
Thatcher's strife
And King Arthur's glorious Flying Pickets

And all in Defence and Aid
Of those at home
Imprisoned and abused
By the absurdity
Of a merciless racial stratification
And the great lumbering cart horse
Of the British TUC
Showing what not to become
To the new emerging giant at home
Intent on Breaking the Chains
Threatening to shake down
Both the shrill desiccated certainties

Of the Cold War apparatchiks
And the comfortable semi-comatose
In their citadels of privilege

Away the cynical secretive securocrats
On both sides
Away then
Away now!
Even from afar
The whiff of compromise
Hung and stung in the air
Coming Home –
How we discussed the possibilities
Of what had to be done!
At picnics
In meetings
At parties
At work
Our jaws ached from talking

But before long
The sharp contrasts that once drove us
Fudged into shades of grey
Grey suits
Grey beards
Grey minds
Polished heads!
And courage was suddenly required
To restate the simplest of changes that were needed
Changes so artfully and convincingly articulated
That for a moment
They were adopted as the norm
But not for very long
As the fearful and vested interests
Exerted and inserted themselves
Preserving only

A once heroic
Once seductive
But now
An empty cloying rhetoric

Being Home –
So many of us were lost along the way
Some of us were not
And used our skills from exile
To became facilitators
Of space
Of enquiry
Of movement
Of surreptitious rebellion
Of an Other Foundation
Even when imprisoned
In a wretched project log frame
It was one way to continue
And we worked hard and did
For as long as we could

Staying Home –
Many of us
Go about our lives
In the not so new dispensation
Bemoaning still
The ugly separateness
In our almost monochrome dinner parties
Our almost monochrome social lives
Can it really be
That only the blurred margins
Of the elite
Have changed?

Always Home –
Most of those old friendships

Forged in the hell that was
Remain welded
And essential
New friendships
Have given encouragement to keep on
To stay outside of luxurious paralysis
To Feel the Ice in the Lungs
To still feel the rumble of movement
Not fully lost
To be alert to possibility
Even when it required
A double shot on the rocks
To really rock!
Heart –
A sibling's child
Leaps into a swimming pool
I watch as a precious god-child
Stretches upwards and overtakes me
And I am alive and happy
This confirms the difference
Between being alone
And being lonely
Never really alone
Given all those
Down down the years
Who have reached out
Keen to ensure
A special continuity
Celebrated today
With an outpouring
Of love
And laughter.

The Wake Today
In more recent times a wake is a social gathering held after a funeral or, in Ireland, often after the death but before the funeral. Traditionally people drink and talk about the dead person, and there is a happy jovial atmosphere.

The Wake in Fluid Dynamics
In fluid dynamics, a wake is the region of disturbed flow (usually turbulent) downstream of a solid body moving through a liquid, caused by the flow of the fluid around it. In incompressible fluids such as water, this results in a wave. As with all wave forms it spreads outward from the source, usually until its energy is overcome or lost by friction or dispersion, but its impact can be considerable and lasting.

(Courtesy of Wikipedia)

Kraal of our Genes

There is an art form only sung and hissed
by those we call the dead.
An art form fixed between poetry and painting:
clay cattle dabbled on river banks not far from eBakhwetheni,
the childhood portraits we drew on the tar-roads of Mdantsane –
all washed out by merciless rains,
scrubbed off by jealous car tyres.

Some say it's an art form to impress the living.
"Wasting time."
That art form is not that far if one truly seeks it.
It is mostly found in kicking imaginary soccer balls,
shadow boxing, ducking and weaving away from imaginary opponents.
It lies hidden on lonely walks, in confronting horizons
and sometimes smiling for no reason and patting one's back.

Listening to crickets or in re-weighing answers
said to be 'best' when scruffling life head on.
An art form tantamount to a man standing
emaxhantini akowayo seemingly doing nothing
but trying hard to convince the full house
yezi Hlwele zakowayo.
Some art is never to be understood.

His Viva's!

One of the most ill-disciplined human qualities is memory.
My father would tell me about his favourite political party
While I was brushing my school shoes or washing the dishes.
A sudden break always snuck in –
His talk mimicked the Israelites in their desert journeys:
Man in true-seek of liberation.
His words would paint like Dumile Feni
With charcoal on fabriano;
So his fantastical narrations heavily fuelled my aspirations
Of being a politician – obviously in his honour.

Then 1994 finally barged in and fumes
Of a 'better living' glowed on his face.
But as time went on, the glow slowly tarnished.
And with all his claims of *nyamezela kwedini,*
I would grind my teeth tighter.
That was up to 2013 and his final years.

How I wish he'd lived to see the dawn of 2016!
Haha . . . *hayi angekhe sbali.*
Forgive me, father, for I've lost trust in your party.
Plainly, just as they purr it, as they mince it,
Feloniously, that "Together we can do more."

Yinyath'uqobo

Ndimva ndikud'enyathela
Ndiv'imvekw'ithule kant'iyozela
Ndimbona ngaphambi kwanax'evuthela
Ndibabona besaba bemnik'indlela

Liqhaji lendoda yinyok'ubulumko
Unamehlw'okhozi undand'emafini
Yinkunz'enkom'uyangcangcazelisa
Yintab'uk'phakama sonke sinamandla

Lixhents'okomXhos'ingesi lakumbona
Ndoyik'okwempukw'emngxunyen'isithele
Ndihlob'okwamas'engekaselwa nguye
Ukhaliph'okwegorha lemfengu lixhobile

Iyamkhahlel'inyosi nayo x'imbona
Luyamthand'ulwandle ngumhlob'alo
Nqandani nants'intlanz'indibulisa
Lamla Nxishaneshe kunts'uk'uthule

Ndincede ndlulamth'undifunqule
Yandil'intlungu lwavuy'uqaqaqa
Kujongil'ukufa noko kundoyika
Rhabul'ufince mfana likhw'ithemba

Ingenil'inyathi zasab'iimvekuba
Yombela mXhos'ifikil'inyathi
Xel'inyhweba ndod'ikhon'inyathi
Nants'inyathi! Imkil'nyathi! Yinyath'uqobo

Umsasazi

Mamelani zindlebe nank'umntw'ethetha
Mayizol'imvul'iphakam'imitha
Lamlani zinkonde kungen'is'helegu
Malihamb'ivila asinandaw'uyak'butha

Yinyosi lo mfo yinkuthalo akalali
Uzilwimi zonkc akakh'osalayo
Nikel'ingqalelo yinkwenkwez'umfo ludumo
Lirharha ngumchukumisi ngumonwabisi

Urhuq'izizw'okwerhamba lifutha
Ukhony'okomqhag'ingesifingo silele
Akanamsil'okwembil'isoyik'utshaba
Unesidima mde okwentlanz'eMeditera

Liyajikajik'ijoni lijiyaza nguye
Ujong'ajam'az'jul'ijacu
Ujij'ijaj'ijik'imjonge
Ndee jezu ndijol'emafini

Udiliz'amazwekazi ngezwi lakhe
Uthetha kunqand'iintsan'eb'thongweni
Uginy'uloliw'unquml'iNcib'imjongile
Ulikhulu lendoda ijol'ezingqaqeni

Uyafundisa uyakhalima noko
Uyalumkisa wena zilumkele
Uyaxhobisa qubul'is'krweq'uye
Uyonwabis'ungalibal'inguye

Lincamil'irhwamncwa

Ifikil'indlovu yancam'uk'gquma
Inxakamil'imaz'enkom'irhaxiwe
Yagqum'ingonyam'isoyikis'abantu
Lihlazekile kuk'ncam'irhwancwa

Babhengezil'abangoyikiyo ndibazi nje mna
Abalal'abeendaba bebik'udaba rhoqo
Azidinw'iindlebe zifun'ithemba malang'onke
Baleka lincamil'irhamncw'ungalityi

Baphuphil'abatsha zalawul'iinkonde
Ibunjiw'ingonyama yaqwenga kwamangalwa
Abharhamlil'amazulu naw'ohluleka
Siyatyhwatyhw'isizwe lincamil'irhamncwa

Maziphum'izinj'azihlal'inabantu
Ibinziw'ingonyam'alikhw'ikamva
Phandan'isilivere magorha nidl'ub'tyebi
Zaphakuzel'iilwandle lincamil'irhamncwa

Zifikil'iintaka kungekh'olindeleyo zadla
Labharh'idlelo lerhamncwa ufil'umfazi
Igcwele yonk'indaw'igolid'akakh'oyifunayo
Lirhale de lancam'irhamncwa ziintloni

Ndibon'ilizwe lihle libukhazikhazi
Yimivuyo abuyil'amaqhaw'ebedukile
Ndimangele ndibon'indod'ivun'entlango
Mka nyhuku nyhuku lerhwamncw'ulizothe

Home address

She refuses to pack and leave
Every morning she prays out loud – twice - while
Standing in front of the massive wooden door
For the third time kneeling in front of the eternal flame

She tells them that the flame is her own fire
That she cooks her meals there and sleeps there on cold nights
That she taught herself to read by standing in front of the lettered door
She tells them that the colossal door is a superwoman
When they say she has lost her mind, she says that is a lie
Her home address is: "Hilltop"
And her name is Dedani.

Tentacles

The tentacles of white men in academia
Go deep, spread wide, entangle
Cross time.
Says a Black woman scholar,
The only solution is to wait
…
…
…
…
…
…
…
…
…
…
for them to die.

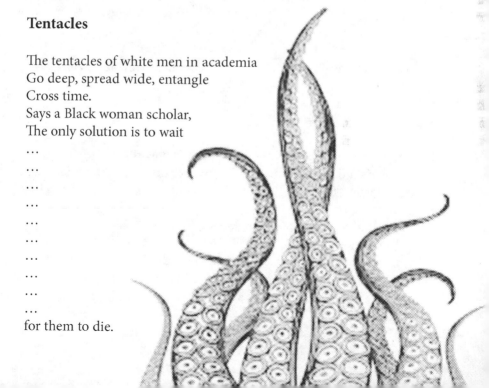

The alkalinity of bottled water

As I pen a poem on the comparisons of alkalinity levels in bottled water
From the distance, I hear the now familiar song: Solomoni! Iyo
Solomoni!
Piercing through the buildings of Braamfontein, unaltered by the
strong winds
From the window of our 7th floor office, we saw the shooting of a
Catholic priest.

The milliequivalents per litre (mVal) of water, commonly known as the
pH
Did these jacaranda trees ever imagine a sight like this, on this site?
In front of the Wits Great Hall: many police vans, black men in police
uniform
Stand with guns in their hands facing a handful of students, singing and
unarmed.

This poem on the alkalinity of bottled water veers to the water we are
sinking into
Parents have not forgotten the words of the minister of higher
education
The words he uttered & then laughed: Students Must Fall! I hear the
sounds of
The struggle tune: Siyaya! Siyaya! These Wits students have not fallen
Not now.

The pH of this water must rise because that is how the body detoxifies
As the ire of students rises throughout the country, as universities burn,
As the minister of finance prepares for his budget speech, as he receives
charges
from the NPA. The rand falls. Anxieties about a possible relegation to
junk status rise.

The mVal of water we have sunk into is falling & we have forgotten that
The CEO of the SABC returned to his job. The news of raging fires, of
burning books!
The end of a seven-year term of the first woman Public Protector this
country has known, is here

The report on state capture is looking for a safe resting place, has had
to wait for court judgement.

As we waver in this water, as we discuss the dangers of this descent
We reach out to our inner core for the power we once possessed, the
power
We once knew we had, in a time we once owned, when the line was
indelible
We now need an end to the welcome disruptions. We welcome the
incoming Public Protector.

While working on this poem on alkalinities, I take a call from a liter-
ary scholar who tells me:
"Apologies the poetry session has been cancelled, no visitors allowed
at the University of Pretoria."

During this period of flaring fires, rising students & conversations
about decolonizing:
Shaeera Kalla. Bullets on you back. Fezekile Ntsukela Kuzwayo. Ten
years later, we look back.

This poem has settled with the analysis of the alkalinity of the water
we are drowning in
As our arms flail in desperation, we hope to start seeing a hard rock
below
Waiting for us at the unfathomable bottom
Fezekile, the four sisters ensured that we never forget: Kufezekile!
And for that, the pH rises and we with it.

As the rock becomes visible, we strengthen our arms & legs, some
pray, others start a song
We dive with smiles on our faces because we realize that the turning
point is close
We would be singing out loud if we were not under water, so we focus
on not drowning
So that we can rise again, resurface and realize the dreams of the de-
mocracy we want.

"The famous south african poet"
(posthumous recognition)

i am no son of the soil
nor daughter of the land
and have no business with mama afrika
my tongue don't click
when i say umkombothi
my throat don't sound like a
cheesegrater when i say
hammanskraal
and i can't use portmanteaus
the way that stephen watson did
i wasn't raised by a strong single mother
don't go to church on sunday
and can't quote from the bible
i have no uncle who died in the struggle
and no schoolmate of mine was shot dead by the cops
(although my aunt nadia drank herself to death
and my friend jim died at 16 of a heroine overdose
and they were freedom fighters
in their own peculiar way)
i had no lover who broke my heart
(although i've been dumped by a few)
my ancestors are people of few words
nothing is happening under my skin
and my blood is very well where it is
as for the stars and the constellations
i don't want them any nearer
and have no message for them
on stage i am soft spoken
i read from the page
and wear no dashiki shirt
i have no youtube channel

no twitter
no instagram account
i have never performed at etv sunrise
never been invited to the franschhoek festival
never been published in prufrock
never been short(nor long)listed
for the sol plaatje award
all i write about is
drunkards
sex
bars
drunkards having sex
and drunkards having sex in bars
one day i shall be a
famous south african poet but
considering the information above
it ain't gonna be soon

another beer, guys?
(written after reading Harriet Sherwood's article "Israelis gather on hillsides to watch and cheer as military drops bombs on Gaza", The Guardian, 20 July 2014)

lead rains have fallen from skies of odium
and starred aircrafts are flying back to hq

amos, shlomo and bram set up their camping chairs
and tables
on the hilltop in front
of the gaza border

they check the iphone batteries: they're full
and so is the portable fridge
the coal in the barbecue is red hot
the golani brigade's banner waves smugly
in the sundown breeze
the stereo blasts
metallica's "kill 'em all"

the buddies uncap three beers
and have a toast

one talmud song and
one selfie
as they wait for the next raid

thuds of shellfire
flashes of explosions
and palls of smoke
from the agonizing strip

"yeah!…" shouts amos
"fuck yeah!" sobs shlomo
"wooooo-ohhhh" grunts bram

a round of hi-tens
and they down the beers

harar and jijiga
warsaw   rotterdam   london dresden
               hamburg   chongqing
guernica   hiroshima nagasaki   philadelphia
   hanoi   beirut belgrade   mururoa
           grozny   kabul   baghdad
      gaza
          gaza
              gaza...

fascists in different eras and
under different flags
have always had a flair for
crashing down cities
bodies
and spirits

their progenies chill on viewpoints with
a hot dog in one hand
and a binocular in the other

and enjoy the show

"there is no rationality in the nazi hatred"
primo levi wrote
"consciences can be seduced and obscured again"
     and again
          and again…

the aircrafts are coming back
the iphones are ready

           "another beer, guys?"

Quintessence

Music flows
Like booze down the throat
Causes a commotion
A moral erosion
Back to back
Front to front
Hips for keeps
Sweetest lips
Tongue-on-nipple
Cause a cosmic body ripple

Umlilo
(Ku David Mmbi)

Iphimbo lakho
Liwumzwilil'ezindlebeni zami
Izwi lakho
Litshiloza okwezinyoni
Emoyeni wami
Umculo wakho
Ungenza ngihlengezele izinyembezi
Eziyimpophoma zenjabulo
Kuqhakaz'izinkanyezi emehlweni ami
Ungibuyisel'enkabeni yeAfrika
Izimpande zakho zizinzile
Ujulil'okwesiziba somful'othelayo
Umculo wakho uzothile, upholile
Buya kimi Afrika, ngabadi yokhokho
Buya ngiphuz'emthonjeni wamanz'akho amtoti.

Da inflashun rate keeps risin
(To LKJ)

Da inflashun rate keeps risin
Eat stale bread without butter
High dreams in a squatter
Sip tea without milk and sugar

Da inflashun rate keeps risin
Babies laboured in a squalor
Next to a funeral parlour
Share water with swine

Da inflashun rate keeps risin
En da prices keep risin
Currency on the low
Like an upset stomach about to blow

Da inflashun rate keeps risin
Powers dat be say
What are you cryin for?
What are you cryin for?

To Bavino Machana

Chant a poem
With a strum of guitar
Drumbeat for sweethearts and the bitter
Ibheshu designed for a griot
Fall back dance of a president
The loot exposed in a riot

We lick an X to the ballot
Freedom dangled like a carrot
Truth on a diet
Poet revolutionary never be quiet
Take a sniper's shot
True verse from the gutter

Uproot the brute
He has overstayed the honeymoon
Wield words like a sword

When women are train stations

❷❺ *Dimakatso Sedite*

I knew a man who had a woman at every station;
each drenched in the perfume of her township,
oozing with the warmth of the bosoms and blankets
of their grandmothers.

Mahikeng fed him hugs;
a sea of a dress flaunting curves,
hiding the hell blazing in her chest
as she swallowed her wrath with a twisted pink-chalked smile.

Orkney wrapped her uneasy hope in tight jeans,
sliding sideways after a few beers gulped in a wind-shocked shack,
too sugar-drunk-sweet to sink into this hollow tube of a man;
a flower blooming in the shadow of a mine dump and loving what
it knew.
(Her boobs, green apples; her nipples, peanuts poking her T-shirt
to a buzz of hooting taxis and GTI's.
Grime of life underneath her cotton-white All Stars,
crushing seeds into the ground.)

Orlando was older, a pot of slow-cooking stew –
simmering his soul as the future waited.
Tembisa was tea, trembling in a paper cup,
trying to tease the Tom out of his train,
tearing its twigs apart to live now and not in Orlando's future
or Mahikeng's anger.

Each station was more than his taste buds could take;
leaving behind snaking smoke to haunt the frozen tracks
of that train of a man.

Bringing Forth

Eve was there
Alone
She had no need for another
She was full breasted

And she lay in the garden
And seeded herself
And her milk made her happy
Eve after Eve after Eve

But when the moon was full and red
A warring rod and whirling light
Disturbed her womb
Till a hard-muscled child pushed out

And so Eve made Adam
Made herself and unmade herself
Made a man to stand
Beside and against her

It is never quiet in the garden
There is always vibration
And still Eve lies alone
Bringing forth Adam after Adam after Adam

Knock- knock

Thut-thut
Can you see him?
The trees are close
Thut-thut
Stop talking
Thut-thut
Time to stop talking
Look up
Listen
Thut-thut
To the woodpecker
Knocking

Knock-ing

Listen!
Listen
To the thut-thut
Trunk
Echo
Echo-ing
With that woodpecker's
Knock-ing

Shh
Stop talking!
Listen
To the thut-thut
Thut
Knock
Knock
Knock-ing

no one is safe

GANG BULLET CASH
that's the one t-shirt
Freedom Dignity
another

in the street

young boys play soccer with a rolled up raincoat
wait for passing cars to get out the way

older majitas slouch by the spaza shop
three toothless women on the stairs
let them suck the baby's milk

and there is music
relentless beat
there is always music coming from the shebeen
in the garage in Phuza Mansions
where an old man shuffles by with his empties

he is afraid of the girls at the corner
you know those three in the basement of Cinnamon Court
he buys them airtime if they'll visit
discretely

across the road from the hair salon
the abandoned building where the homeless
make use of the ceiling
lights up every night

the flicker of these fires
fires the imagination
NO ONE IS SAFE FROM THE GANG THAT COMES
OVER THE WALLS

the old man shuffles
sees rats tails on the kitchen tiles

inside the mayoral office the mayor
repeats reports about urban decay
the media broadcast his policy:
no surrender to the mafias

foreigners ARE responsible

the boys playing soccer do not see the official sedan

the man behind the wheel
steers it away from the scene

lucky the media were asleep in their hammocks
lucky there is no one to video the pantie's on the car seat
the mayor's open bottle of heavenly spirits

the youngest boy is in the gutter
neck broken on impact
the oldest boy is crying
the ball has popped and the game exploded

now clouds shade the street

and as the weather turns
the old man shares his wisdom
he is a guy who dreams

he confirms   no one is safe from the gang that comes over the walls
no one is safe
but the biggest crooks are the white collar brigade
who sell you insurance

truly
there's no point trying
to play safe
by living   in a safe

Psychiatric emergency

Boredom smells damp
the floor rises to her tongue
sits there, a throbbing molar
she's grateful for the pain
the waiting room no oasis
the grey walls won't engage
the vinyl chair cracked from agitated bums
agitates hers
morsels of the day

pincered by sunlight
skim lino floors
scabbed by tooth and nail
and the empty eyes of
those who have seen
green grass recently
now fast fading to black
to zero tolerance
for being where
the ceiling is glaze-eyed

where hands hang
lifeless things
even when a scream
drops into the thirsty air
lands in a smudge on the floor
like a secret she cannot divine
though she feels it wormy
beneath her inauthentic skin

she closes her eyes
feels her shoulder blades in
the palms of your hands
that ancient summer
when you and she and
dope and Jimi Hendrix
once exonerated yourselves

Sleep

Stippled with light
my grown son
splayed like some inert
sun-drenched amphibian
in a disorder of
limbs and linen
clutches at sleep
with clenched fists
squeezes from it
oblivion like a love affair
without peaks or plateaus

leprechaun memory
tousles his hair
freckles his nose
flashes the grin
of a small boy
turned fugitive from
outsize dreams

An Inheritance

I don't remember how it began
with water or without?
with trembling or without?
satisfied or fainting?

How might we measure it?
the dregs of a season
one white confetti bush
the salt on your hands
an armchair
honeyed in winter light

Did we sigh for the ease of it?
Did we think ourselves free?

As though our mothers are not ghosts
As though this language is not
a haunting

There is a power in calling a thing by its proper name

Not 'infidelity'
Let us say
a history of disappearance
Let us say
men forget their names

Not 'a Black man hits his
Black wife'
Let us say
she is alone in a room
Let us say

she is a rose in bloom
What of your names?
he who came by water
and blood
bright edge of the knife
worn-knot of breath
bees in the throat

What to Say to the Immigration Officer When He Ask You Where You Are From

Say you left in a hurry
say the days stumbled
blind
say the high grasses
swallowed the raw-boned women
feeding babies
in the field

Say you were
twenty-two in all
say half were lost in
the first week
say you prayed to
die young
say you lived on
and on

Say the belly of the dry
season
say the lash of the earth
say you swallowed
whole countries
say you spit only ash

An Ode to Soap

here is
the breath
of paper wrapping

                        the soft rustle
                of prayer

for the swelling
in the knees
for two small bruises
on the breast
for the air at first light
hungry and roaming

here is
the first clean bite
of mint
quince pear on the windowsill
the slow aria of vanilla
the notes so open
you could weave
the sweetness
in

here is
the white porcelain bowl
the daydream of water
skin the colour
of baked nectarines
in the bleached sea light

here is
the wet grass
the heaven
and the earth
the bright throat
of spring
yawning across
the sky

The Serious Moonlight

2 9 *John Carse*

i am a lover
of the serious moonlight
the solemn pleasure
of the rose
and the ugly criticism
of the early morning light
that makes me doubt

i love
not only the pretty things
the sparkling baubles
of your occasional kisses
the soft seductive touches
of your eyes
i love too
your lies

it's twisted i know
but when you lie to me
i think that you still care
enough to hide the truth
it is your youth
that bruises my age
your rotting love
that abuses me

Vuka Muntu Omusha

Vuka ubone muntu omusha.
Vuka wenze muntu omusha.
Vuka kuzwakale muntu omusha.
Vuka ubonakale muntu omusha.

Impilo yakho iphethwe nguwe,
Ikusasa lakho lisezandleni zakho.
Impumelelo yakho yakhiwa nguwe.
Injabulo yakho yakhiwa nguwe.
Ithemba lakho libe kuMdali.

Vuka muntu omusha.
Vuka uyibambe.
Vuka uphokophele.
Ikusasa lakho alingafani nezolo lakho.

Wena uyithemba lesizwe.
Wena uyikusasa lesizwe.
Wena unguvela bahleke.
Wena uyenza kwenzeke.
Ungakwenza kulunge.

Amathuba ayimbaba,
Amakhono angangolwandle,
Imfundo ngeyamahhala,
Amabhizinisi ayavulwa.
Vuka muntu omusha.

Wena awufani nokhokho,
Wena awufani nomndeni wakho.
Amalungelo angakuwe,
Phuma phambili qhawe.
Vuka muntu omusha.

Themba Lami

Themba lami lokugcina,
Wena ngikubiza ithemba lami lokugqina,
Ngoba elokuqala lafika langishiya.
Ubuhlungu sebuphelile ingqondo ayisoze yakhohlwa.
Kepha inhliziyo seyixolile.

Bethanda bengathandi noma umhlaba ungangenza inhlekisa,
Kepha mina ngizobambela kuwe kuhle kohlanya.
Ngizonamathela kuwe kuhle kweshungami inamathele ekhanda.

Angikuthandi njengami,
kepha ngikuthanda njengawe uthanda mina.
Uma ngishiya wena kuyobe angiyazi into engiyenzayo,
Kuyomele ngithule ngingakhulumi lutho ngothando,
Ngoba wena uwuthando uqobo.
Sthandwa somphefumulo wami uma ngishiya wena kuyobe ng-
ishiya impilo yami uqobo.

Themba lami ngithathe ungithande,
Ngimi phambi kwakho ngiyababaza,
Hha ngomlomo,
Kepha ngenhliziyo nangothando.,

Saphela Isizwe

Saphela isizwe sakithi,
Saphela isizwe esimnyama,
Sapkela isizwe sako Madiba,
Saphela isizwe sakwethu.

Bashabalala abahlobo bethu,
Zahamba izithandwa zethu,
Saphela isizwe sakwethu.

Ingabe yini le ebulala isizwe kangaka,
Ingabe yini le egwinya isizwe sakwethu,
Bahamba abadumile,
Bahamba abangaziwa,
Saphela isizwe sakwethu.

Bahamba abakholwayo,
Bahamba abangakholwa,
Ingabe mhlaba wenziwani,
Usuqeda isizwe kangaka,
Sesiyaphela isizwe sakwethu.

Solitude

Which census will count
my hands desire? Which
government official the
parabellum of your body,
smooth and brown and wet
in air, within air, moving
into fading sunlight?

The lucid intervals of speech
that quiver. The small
touch of your fingers, invisible
to the punctured beliefs. A
mountain fell on the musk,
pain blinked in veins,
roots stirred in political hunger.
Why such vulnerability?
Leaning against a wall,
words lost in need.

There was silence between the windows.
I comb the blind flesh nervously,
counting renegade dreams.
The real evil is belief in perfection.
The hungry plague climbs the spine's stair,
in air, within air.

There

There are those spiritually hungry
who should be left alone
to be allowed to suffer
and fight for the self
their way
and not become colonised objects
of pity in the news
or tomorrow's anthropological
thesis.

There are those who are lonely
who hunger for a god
that still won't be named
or mirrored in human alphabet
or given a particular face
except the face
of everybody.
They should never be hidden
from loneliness
or given a place
where they will be hidden
from the tragedy
of reality.

It should enter them
in the eyes
in all the curved horizons
it will return to them
they will recognise it
in all directions
where they see
tangible living truths
that keep changing shape
because truth is a living thing

like a rainforest or
a colony of ants
or a stream of mountain water
or a compound of people
a low cost housing project
a taxi with a sliding door
a man selling chips
your barefeet hardened
by years of walking
old newspapers
and not a word
or somebody's pure idea
it is here
and it moves
keeps moving
moving.

There are those who evangelise millions
and have never fallen in love
or been intimate with one person
or even slightly aware
that the self
keeps dying
somewhere inside the mirror
and all photographs
that are being taken by the media
are images of that which
has already died
and become another.

But none of this really makes me unhappy anymore.
Not even the peace in your eyes I will never fully understand.
There's too much restlessness in my love.
This moment I am yearning for you doesn't have to end soon.

City Buzz

Johannesburg

Becoming a truly African city -
which it has been, but not for all
and perhaps not African in the eyes of many
not African in lifestyle, even if in Africa

Johannesburg

Bursting with curiosity, the urge to discover
what it doesn't yet know
the urge to be on a par
with Lagos, Dar es Salam, Addis Ababa
not really Cairo but perhaps Casablanca
Jozi-Alex-Soweto - beyond Casablanca!

Johannesburg

A destiny quite distinct from that of Cape Town
more urgent
taking more risks
steppin' out
daring to show and share
über-urban

Contradictory

Johannesburg

Do I have to betray my father to love you?
Or are there no betrayals in love?
Perhaps he loved you just as much
Without knowing you as I do

Under the Southern Cross
4th Sept 2016, BA flight JHB-London

I leave
by crescent moon
lights below reflecting the high life
while absence of light may reflect the low life

The country is almost 22
a youth
attempting to find its way

Within it
      those who have had it all (despite exceptions)
      those still dreaming
those who can participate in the dialogue:
the artists
the business people
the entrepreneurs
the office holders
the workers
the students
the teachers

There is a desire to live in a new, changed country

There is mistrust of the time it takes

I come from the Old Guard
the Protected
my father thought that change would be for foreign power
an invasion he would fight

Yet I feel hope
I feel proud

There are Voices

I would like to be one of them.

Mysterious Girl

3 **3** *Lisa-Marie Labercensie*

Some refuse to understand my protest because of my mysteries.

There was a time when I thought people failed to show me acceptance,
but now I understand
I am the one who is supposed to accept my differences,
my own mystery.

Some ignored my heart's language – it is up to me to teach them.
It is up to me to study my heart's language.
Sometimes I find my mysteries lead me to wonder if I'm doing enough
but I know me and my mysteries have promised each other
to do everything for the ones we love.

If we fail for our bull's eye
we will not give up.
I will not give up.
I am a mysterious girl.

I need no make-up.
I need no shadows to hide my scars, I am proud of them.
They show I stood up.
They show I cared.
I need no money to prove that I can walk that mile you think I can't.

Don't ever underestimate the power of a mysterious girl.
I need not hide behind a glass of rum or a stick of smoke.
Me and my mysteries are strong enough to stand on all ground,
not hiding, not crying.
Simply waiting.

This Last Embrace in Darkness

3 4 *Josephine Bonaparte*

This last embrace in darkness
A false night
Before a homicidal dawn.
My arms around your neck
Fingers grasping rapaciously at your hair
Your noose leeching from my throat
Futile shadows of despair.

A sepia filter shrouding this montage
In defiant serenity;
A meagre shield
Against swords of light
Poised
To burn through the bodies
Of those carrying the blight.

A door begins to lift
A subtle groan of nascent sunshine
And, impaled
My limbs slacken
Forcing me to my knees
Which meld to the ground.

You have not met a poet

③⑤ *Unathi Slasha*

You have not met a poet yet
Until you come across the warrior womb-man
That goes to war with an infant on her back
She gets letters of threats
As a Christmas gift
From the powers that be

You have not met a poet
Like you have not met God
The tribal orator
His spoken word guides
Like harangues and rebukes to the child
Like sunlight and irrigation to the seed
Like manure it stimulates
The growth of the nation

You have not met a poet
If he calls himself one
Yet speaks the subtle language of the serpent
Then sells his brethrens to the lowest bidder
If he seeks to make minions out of humble men
Belittle then exploit them like Uncle Sam
Degrade their womb-men
Then tread upon them with dusty feet

You have not met a poet
If he makes millions from selling moonshine
That inebriates the public
To lose the sense of freedom and onus
You have not met one
If you have not spoken with a person
That speaks his mind

With a sharpened tongue that cuts through lies
Paves a path through the congested bushes
Preventing the black nation
From adamantly clinging to liberation
The true tribal bard burns his suits then cut his ties with the West

You have not met a poet
If he still writes love letters to the government begging for change
Or is afraid to pinpoint the corruption of Malema
And how the president is lame
How our Heroes wiped their arses with the Freedom Charter
Or if he trembles when speaking
About the effects brought by the legacy of Madiba and Others
That got most gulping the scraps of whites in dumpsters

You are yet to meet a poet
That approaches the stage with Molotov cocktails
Then opens his mouth to fire shots
With a voice that equates the sound
Of thunderclaps
His words are a storm that stops
Daily negative operations
And activities that are do not benefit the community
He writes eulogies to black unity
Then recites a lament to the fallen
Preparing funeral arrangements for whitism
And her counterparts

You are yet to meet a poet
With the fiery breath of an angry dragon
That coughs and spits flames to the Baas and his Madam
Cursing and handing out 'Voetsek' tokens to
The ones responsible for his social bedlam
Stampeding upon their seeds
Uprooting their creed from our soil

You are yet to meet that poet

13 April 2006 before the Passover eve

All biza play en no thesha
reduces jacky to
a madala boy
koppie dice no drakes
from one street corner to corner
all binge en puffing
change pozi
before the Passover eve
sunrise parade
thru the streets of Soweto
dawn until dusk while
all binge en puffing mjucate
kwaito sound splash
kha vhari xwa ngeno
hune vhanwe vhatshiamba
vhanga vho hadzingelwa
mathuthu mulomoni
before the Passover eve

(hurry up and lean this side
where other people speak
as if someone fried
popcorn in their mouth)

I am not

i am not a roadblock
striker busted or
a steep slope
searching slide sethoba mazenke
forcevuur trigger jazzman star black pajero
suffer gate mourn malombo kite

i am not a flatroller thesha spin
tricycle green belt tsingandededze
by en bye
even in high vista rows
thiza ntanjane blazer phola cap
banana kar stork sweets badge
dorpenaar topshaela or molaola siphithiphithi
traffic cop sefate

i am not a town hall speedometer ball
trinity joke
in times of your life span
or a wheelbarrow crank
fix it all tick toes tick
foul feet take your times en fry

i am not

Elelwani N. P Muila (Oct, 1984)

ranga u thetshelesa ngeno
iwe mafuka duvha
u nembelela ha shamba
asi u wa halo
vhe tshikwatamba tsha luranga
ponze ifa yo nambatela mulivho
vho muvhuya phedza dza nga
ndi luvha nga ndothe
musanda a thiluvhelwi
a huna gota
li no luvhela linwe
la u tavhela u li ore
matshelo
liyo tavhela vhanwe vho
naledzani ndi muila
phalalani tsengela tsiwana
fhasi dzi thavhani
vhu ima mbidi na khongoni
phalalani muila matavhelo
buka li sa ori duvha
muthannga musekene
mutamba na vhokunaho
muthannga a sa li vhutete
ngau shavha u tetemela
muila tshivhindi tsha nguluvhe
a sa li phinimini
muila thende ya lufheto
wa thumbu
i nou phangwa mahe
mutavha ya xa
heke..,kha la venda

*

In remembrance of N.P Muila (Oct, 1984)

listen here first
you who wear the sun
the dangling of a wild fruit
does not mean it is falling down
the hard core stalk of a pumpkin stem
dies attached to the mother plant
those who play smart with my flock of cattle
i worship on my own
in the royal house no one who worships for me
there is no headman
who worships for the other headman
if the sun rises and shines on you go for it
tomorrow the sun rises and shines for others as well
no rejection is sacred
rescue and save the poor
down in the mountain valley
down near the station of wild animals and zebras
rescue sacred midday sunshine
which animal does not bask in the sun
a slim gentleman
who baths with pure ones
a gentleman who does not eat soft porridge
cause of fear to shake
a white liver is sacred to him
he who does not eat a parrot
a handle tip of a stirring spoon is sacred to him
with a tummy
which when splashed with sand
remains flat
yeah right.., Venda

Translation by Mboneni Ike Muila

Beach (for Leiga)

1.

The pull of the wash, the wind at your head, the sea calls
in a sheer voice that tips Big Bay like a blue glass plate,
twirls everything for one moment, lovely
plate on a fingertip, spinning the day,
the long mountain with its urban scratchings,
the whole edge of this place,
even these major commercial developments
behind the dunes, come blurring past my right ear

at gentle speed; this power
I can concede, this
shameless kind of life.

Only the boats, tankers, vacant cargo carriers,
blocky liners and little sails, accents, rests,
keep to their lines out there, I could probably write
a lightweight piece for guitar in that space
if I had the music.

2.

We walk back
against the wind, the hard sandgrains

like grease on the skin,
must be some oil
in the air, but then again

perhaps just
sunblock number 3
for you,
Vaseline Intensive Care
for Men, for me.

All dogs look like Snoopy (the Red Baron)
in this wind. We weave along
avoiding the edge, bow to the sand,

there's a graded order here,
such an easy transition from ultrafine to raw
as they dry and stiffen when the wave retreats
and these smooth dark pearly grey
stones inviting desire, yearn to be chosen,
carried home to the garden, perfect
for the human hand.

Sleep (for Megan}

In the dream Megan and I were sleeping
on the stoep of a shop on the main road
under one grey woollen blanket. It was morning
not cold, comfortable. I thought let's go into
the house upstairs, but she said no Dad
I'm warm here. She was right of course
even without the mattress. Those days
we could be comfortable anywhere.

No public opinion, maybe. Warm on the inside.
We could easily slip the time zones.
One other time we went to thornton rd
to watch the crowds. Spectacular siege
of Sinton students one morning the police
teargassed every one, and we ran but
she was always safe in time and space
never too distant. There were days, even weeks
we wouldn't see each other. They
were like unbroken music; for a long time.

Then came the dark period, call it night
call it memory, or a journey, a birthing and again one,
years of packing and unpacking; multi-coloured
clothing, the growth of many houses, huge
maturation of cities and satellite populations.
In sleep now there's often a man, always clothed
and we argue. Two nights ago we fought.
I strangled him. The songs are coming back.

Lefaseng la rena

Lefaseng la rena moratiwa,
Dithabeng tše dikgolo tša lerato
Mo dipelo tša rena di bethago ka mošito o tee.
Megopolo le dihlologelo di abelanago maikutlo.
Dikakanyo di swanago ebile ditšhumelana.
Nokakgolo ya lerato e ya elela ka bokgabo.
Go kgabisa le go nošetša matšoba lefaseng le.
Dinonyana di letša melodi ya dipina tša thekgo.
Go tiišetša Khutšo Lerato lefaseng la rena.
Lefase le apere botala-morogo
Botse bja hlago bo hlatsela dipopo tša gago naletšana ya ka.
Ruri, o tloga o le sebabola o phala le matšoba a naga.

Digagabi lefaseng le ditletše segwera le pelonolo ya lerato.
Dibapala Khutšo le kgwerano.
Lefase la moswananoši la maatlakgogedi
Kgopolo ya ka e phela e fodile bjalo ka metse a sediba.
Ke kgona le go raloka papadi ya ka ya polelo.
Ka boledišana le lona lefase le ka le tsikiritla ka kgona go lokologa go
ntšhetša leino la moseo.
Go realo la nkutulela diphiri le makunutu a lona.

Lefaseng le go rena khutšo
Go rena tokologo ya mogopolo.
Lefaseng la babedi wa boraro ke mpheane
Lefase la go hloka selabi
Lefase la tshephišo le gosasa go go kaone.
Borutho le setšhabelo sa ka dikgatelelong tša monagano.
Lefase le le mpotša ditaba tša go hlarolla madi a mmele le mogopolo.
Mo ke agilego dintlo tša mabatobato
Dikepe tša moya di sepela lewatleng la lefase le.
Defofane di fofa ka nyakalalo di dira lefase le gore le be le mohlaba.
Tšohle di sepela marediredi ka thelelo ya dithelelo.
Lefase la go se tsebe tshele le manyami.

Therešo

Ke nna nokakgolo-moela ka boitshepi,
Ke bolela bophelo bja mmakgonthe
Ke nna therešo ke imela ba maaka
Bo ramaaka le mo mmamaaka ba nhloile
Gobane ke nna makhura
Ke moetapele wa maleba
Leleme la ka ke la boleta la tshepišo
Ke nna kgonthe-a kgodia-kgookgoo
Ke a tšhabega eupša ke a phediša
Boleng bja ka bo godimo
Ga ke segasege le bohwirihwiri
Bokalajane ga re nwešane meetse
Pipamolomo ga e nyake le go mpona
Gobane wa ka molomo a ka se o pipe
Ke nna therešo ke sepela thwii!!!
Ge ele ditselana tša magotlo ga re sepelelane
Ge ke boletše ke boletše
Megabaru le bojato ge ba mpona ba hlanola direthe
Lehloyo le meferefere ba nhlompha ka hlompho ya bod-
itšhabatšhaba
Gobane maatla a ka a roba sekala
Nna kgoši gare ga dikgoši
Ga ke na lebadi la bosodi le ga nnyane
Le ge o ka nnyakišiša o senya metsotso ya gago
Ke tsela yeo e lokologilego ga ena manyofonyofo
Ke moya-mokgethwa sesepela leseding
Ge e le mogwera ga ke naye
Ga ke tšee lehlakore
Nna therešo seimela leleme la bofora
Bontši ba re maaka a phološa nnete ea bolaiša
Maaka a phološa nakonyana yona yeo
Gomme gosasa ga makhura gwa ikgetha

Maaka ga a sepele leeto le le telele
Maaka ga a na boleng
Maaka ga a age motse
Maaka a bopa motho wa go se itshepe
Nnete e phela go ya go ile
Therešo e botse ebile e bose
Ditšhaba di a ntuma eupša ba palelwa go phela le nna
Malapeng monna le mosadi ba khutelane
Ba phela ka go radiana
Ba tlaišana gobane ga ba na therešo
Ba tshepišana gomme ba se phete
Lerato la bofora ga se lona
Ba patlamelane ba ipitša gore ke ba lapa
Lapa le nyaka motheo wa therešo
Tshepano le lerato la mmapale
Therešo e aga lapa la go tia
Therešo e tswala katlego
Lethabo ya ba setšo sa rena
Gomme Khutšo ya ikgweranya le rena

how dangerous they are, the actors!

3 9 *Sjaka S. Septembir*

how dishevelled are their spines of diamond!
how far back their breaths extract nourishment
suckling on the feet of Socrates and that lot.
have you seen them? they have the bodies of spies.
look how loaded that female actor is!
breasts heaving mortar rockets, her nipple points are
secretly hollowed to shatter on impact and
rip the innards of its victim to shreds
they are not human! look
how deformed that male actor-thing is, sprouting
heads of mask and his phallus mocking Christ
Allah, Buddha, everything holy.
keep them away these actors! don't allow
their napalm shadows to touch you!
they will come at you through the gentle hand of TV
their stare secretly feeds us with orange torture
when we just want to forget and laugh
when we want to be free – their laughter secretly lures us
away from the play parks of sanity…
i cannot explain this but i have a feeling,
i just know this is happening, so
beware! beware!
how dangerous they are, the actors!
but where can we run my friends?
where will we find valleys of peaceful shopping?
'coz these actors are fucken everywhere, man.
they stare down at us from every screen with underlying
Big Brother cynicism and in our dreams they stare at us
with the cold hatred of ghosts. we're just not aware . . .
nowadays even my friends babble in my ears
about the world being a stage and
'you should have seen'…this happened in this movie, and

that happened in that movie and NOTHING HAPPENS IN
THEIR OWN LIVES anymore . . . and
everyone is catching this acting disease
delirious with fever they come to act in your life!
i see them re-enacting scenes, lines, from sitcoms
keep them away! keep them away!
they are all secretly growing thangs
flee! run for your lives!
arm yourselves!
yeah, beware of the actors, man . . .
they're growing second souls
i'm warning you,
beware, my friends beware . . .

sello

4 0 *Zama Madinana*

who said sello is dead
coz he lives in the quiet violence of dreams
he tells tales of tormented souls
& deciphers the hidden stars
dangling under azanian skies
he charms you
to dig from the pages of his fiction
he is immortal like dambudzo
he is the undying lyrical wizard
he is a soldier of literature

Music is our pain, and our pain is our music

music is the accidental
uncomfortable sound
when we bite our tongues

when our bones crack
like bird-skulls in
sixty degree heat spells

when telephone lines
screech as they crease the dial
when the waiting subsides
and your heart changes tides

the sound of greetings
breaking like
iron engulfed in raging flames
who will remember all the names?

the sound of regretting
wakes them up like a canon in the morning
the sound of a million hearts
echoing awkwardly against the sunrise
and slowly

the melody is pain
pain is the rhythm in the melody

Dragon Monologues

Twenty-seven and a half cigarettes
Later, and you
Think I'm still
Overdosing on those
Stellar-gone-ballistic somersaults through
The circles of your corduroy heart,

Perhaps

You think I still keep my ego
In the backbone of some
Flame-spitting dragon,

Don't you?

As only your weight knows
The feel of my most fragile shove,
As only you had seen
Enough of my skin-shedding
In the death-kiss minute,

Limping toward the door with your
Heart hangin' from
Your wrist and your
Eyes obscured by netherworld mist,

Like a robed eagle; sixty-winged
Absconder, doin' away
With the former, yet
Unsure of the latter, fallin'
Into your own hardened charisma, while

Some of my catharsis is
Tossed into
The deep creel of moon
Captors,

But I am not still
Locked up in the
Escapade; moving
My shadow along any castle-looking
Wall and holding
The weapons of my own
Injury in my hands, as

If I know nothing about
Impact and bandaging, and
All the other disappearing
Drops of blood, escaping through
The glitches in my logic

Like some stirred up
Cup of dementia, spilling
Over, onto the foundation

Four hands laid down
Themselves, by some volition
Now bludgeoning itself
Against the added barriers,
And all those finger-caressing silences,

Now

Because you've always thought
Of utopia as
Dystopia, so curled
Into your errors, some glabrous
Tree will bear all the wrong fruit,

And I, I am ambiguous
As the thrid fountain coin, draggin'
On my cigarette under water, then
Blowin' all the misery out with the
Wet clouds of departing smoke,

And proving you wrong, every
Time you think I lose my sleep
For you, by

Waking up the rain
Clouds in your sky.

Tiptoed
(For Gabeba Baderoon)

4 1 *Phelelani Makhanya*

Silence is the siren of the night
Words take off in lullaby wings
Breaking locks of quarantined hearts
Her fluffy voice painting shrines
Where butterflies marry stars
Where dreams intercept
Nightmares before they
Reach our bedroom doors.

She removed her sandals
Refusing to stamp the soil
Tiptoed gently and slowly
Passing heaven's tinted windows
Yet making their curtains
Move like swings in a park.

4 2 *Three poems by JOOP BERSEE*

Hiraeth – Three poems for my mother 1923 - 2012
Hiraeth /hIəraI Ө/ is a Welsh word that has no
direct English translation. However, the University
of Wales, Lampeter, attempts to define it as home-
sickness tinged with grief or sadness over the lost or
departed.

Mine, hers?

My mother is her hands.
She sits like Buddha and
plays with a few fingers,
looking at them. First

there were cobwebs
between her old fingers.
Now they are gone;
slowly she wakes up

inside me and starts to
open the cupboards and
becomes young again
as she lives between the

hairs of my eyelashes,
bending, what do I see,
or what does she see
through my eyes, hers?

Star

Yes well we are distant now,
the past like a darkening wall
between us, an illness. I
touch the bricks with my fingers,
break my nails as I try to
scratch the cement, grey, bitter,
can't focus any longer.

Her images are coming
out of my chest, projected
on the wall like good old slides,
the images seem to be soft,
soft toys, a cushion with
her photo on it. A star.

Thank You

Yes she died, dead,
really,
when I put her ashes,
her dust, true kiss,
into the ground,
hole.

No matter,
because a mouse
dies and who
are we, writers,

painters, police man,
baker, pizza maker?
They put ashes into our hands.
Thank you.

Now we, too, ride in limousines

❹❸ *Matthews Phosa*

Now we, too, ride in official limousines.
And humbly get:
Yes-master
Yes-sir
Yes-minister
Yes-everything.
The 'no' people of the struggle have learned
'Yes' habits swiftly and without explanation.

We have become part of the history we fought against.
We are the Establishment!
We created the most unequal society on earth.
Everything that happens in this country is a direct result of what
we think,
how we behave and conduct ourselves and the attitudes we choose.

Aph'amaqhawe?
Where are the ones for whom we have been waiting?
Everyone has returned from exile and prison.
Nelson Mandela's spirit was released more than 25 years ago.
None but ourselves can claim our place.
We are our own liberator.
We are our own oppressors.

your mother is just your mother

44 *Khadija Sharife*

your mother is just your mother
cool hand on the burning forehead,
steaming basmati rice on fridays,
but she is also
revolution,
bodies broken into words forming sentences that function as cages
she is the wrong side of the struggle, built right-side up
inside, where nobody goes
she is five locks on the door with keys clutched in sweaty palms
shadows behind the windows and tapped phones
(even now, got milk is 'coming home soon';
even now, the word 'alone' is not to be mentioned)
she is two sets of grandparents,
the real and the believed, pictures of homes with no addresses
postcards with no names; and multiple beginnings;
where monsters are people are shapeshifters,
your cousin, your father
 - you?
and whispered lullabies never to trust anyone
including her.

Portrait of the poet as young woman

Her hair
Freshly harvested dreadlocks
Unedited gospel of love
Off limits to combs.

Tresses like streams
Of eternal fire
From the arsenal of her body.

Poems conceived in a celestial tongue
When stars align with caesarean precision.
It is our own language.

Her verses
Are neither left nor right aligned.
Time zones hinge at every line break
Like sunflowers UN-aligned to the scorching heat.

Every evening on her terrace
She lets her hair down and flies kite.
Her verses tell vivid stories
Stitched together in myriad colors.

Her verses gurgle like rivers let loose.
She never braids them
With her bare hands
Before a poetry reading.

When her poems are read
No boyfriend or pimp is allowed
Inside the reading hall.

Her kite, untethered to her surname,
Soars high till it gets entangled with the stars.

Attempting to translate her poems
Is like making love to a capricious mistress.

Untamed by the clanging of her anklets,
Her curly kinky stream of verses
Sways to the rhythm of her gait.

Her book of poems –
a treatise on 'dishevelled hair'
and tresses on fire.

Caste in a Local Train

Caste in a local train can be deceptive
like the soul of a Pakistani fast bowler
camouflaged in a three piece suit
and an Anglicized accent.
Seated opposite,
I feel him start his charge
towards me.

If my surname is too long,
I could be caught behind.
Will I be trapped leg-before-wicket
if I attempt a bloodline crossover?
I try to hide behind
stripes of concocted ancestry
pushed along by fresh water currents.
Can I switch over to
my mother's surname
using the active/passive voice
in the midst of a harangue?

I sit back,
hope I do not lose my nerve
at the bouncers of abrasive queries.
I try to find myself a place
in his skull beyond his caste mark,
between his eyebrows:
trying to find my way around
an ever changing map!

He tries assessing me with an inswinger:
"What is your full name?"
Then he tries an outswinger that seams a lot:
"And what is your father's name?"
By this time, he loses his patience
And tries a direct Yorker –
"What is your caste?"

I was in love with a psycho

4 6 *Phozisa Mkele*

The colours were yellow
The day
It never really was daytime
Signs of friction that took a silver colour
My heart was blood
Gushing red upon red
Dirty red upon red
A waste of good donor blood really
Left to its own devices
On a ceramic tile
Soaked by an inexpert Mr. Price towel
If the towel was that soiled then how must my insides have
looked?
Like a street side abortion
. . . I'm guessing.

The colours are still yellow
Those are the official colours
The colours we vote for

I was in love with a psycho
(I want to lie and say was)
But I would describe this love as something daddy never finished
So I learnt to love incorrectly
And pretend to be loved back incorrectly
I'm grateful for the gesture
However small
IN LOVE WITH THE PSYCHO
Ergo: Becoming the psycho.

Holy Day

4 7 *Anna Varney-Wong*

mom is watching the rain
drops dropping
counting her days
on her counter
1st this way then that
watching the passing train
rat-a-tat-tat-tat
rat-a-tat-tat-tat
a lit window, a lit window
window, window, window
rat-a-tat-tat-tat
rat-a-tat-tat-tat
a rapist is pounding
gra-anna's body
which she left
again and again
boom boom boom
it's not hail, it's not a hammer
it's a rock falling down the mountain
on these bodies in this land
of the living
where we're all dead

my husband a-lights
to pinch my cheeks
he cries, 'pinch the mooon!!!'
it's all colours
beach balls bouncing
bounce bounce bounce
in this land of mirrors
where we think we must think
to understand living

in this land of the dead
have you noticed
how close 'alone' is to all-one?

the mantra beads clink in the morning
clink clink clink
tryambakam*:
when the time is right
the ripe cucumber falls from the vine:
may we be free from attachment
free free free
my mother is counting the rain beads
clink clink clink

at last the chance came
to cut the umbilical cord
where we were hanging
strung to the tree
setting us free free free
ashes are candles on the Ganga
taking this chance
to be free free free

the rain falls gently

Identity (crisis)

4 8 *Linda Loubscher*

You
who assume I'll laugh at your slightly racist joke
(which isn't even funny)
and expect me to agree that the country is going to the dogs
(because you believe incompetence and corruption come only in
black)

I'm not like you

You who sway from side to side with a vierkleur flag around your
shoulders
singing De la Rey De la Rey with religious fervour

or wear T-shirts with the slogan
praat Afrikaans of hou jou bek

I don't like you

And you who talk about protecting
and supporting
our language
our culture
'our people'

I am not your people

Yet
because my ancestors arrived in Cape Town three centuries ago
and I have a surname that can't be pronounced in English
because of the pale freckledness of my skin

the accent I speak with
the language I dream in

because language (by association)
becomes a culture of Reitz four khaki pants 7de Laan bokkie
rokkie sokkie music

like a gangrene limb I can't amputate

suddenly

I am you

White-gilt

④⑨ *Kirby Mania*

While kids
comb the shore (for
seashells/pebbles/deadcrabs),
the adults
cross the sandy strip
to fill empty coke
bottles with
seawater.

Wiping before their
eyes, the holiday
a black-and-white
slideshow (dotted with
technicoloured
redball/yellowspade/greenstripedumbrella)

In fourbyfours now (beachsand
caught in candyflosshair,
trappedbetweentoes/stuckinseams/crumbedpockets),
they tackle
the halfday journey home
passing ultracities and themed playgrounds
(with goats/pigs/chickens in pens),
stippling the landscape
allthewayback
to the golden city.

Sitting quietly,
the coke bottles filled
(sandwichedbetween
suitcases/spades/woolworthspackets)

They are
tenpins, upright
as a conscience
appeased.

The Question of Nocturnal Carnations

5 0 *Hyun-Jung Anna Kim*

So a Neruda the Brownings
black-and-white photograph of the head of a guitar later
we arrive
at a round table of six
a languorous Sunday South African lunch
no matter

complexities
murmurs of the human heart
memories
whirl unspool in the human mind
layers upon layers
webs of half-truth half-question

the long language*
spoken heard
silence beyond silence
a question beside a question
without unhinging impinging

a different point of emphasis
nocturnal flowerings
leaves of carnal fruits
seaweed crushed in mud and light
furtive declensions into starry waters.

Sad

5 **1** *Mbali Mashiya*

Nowadays there are certain 'things' one should have
Batho haba da hore wa khomba kappa o khwela cab,
Just as long as you make it to the party on Friday night
O shebe ho nowa bo Tox, Storm, Brutal fruit …. E seng sprite

It's normal to find a 16 year old girl rock up at party uninvited
Aitse skinny sa Guess, a floral shirt, carvella ka side bag ya Louis
Vitton
Leteng, a jola motho wa taxi
So don't get a fright,
Ungasabi . . .

Bloemstas are already used to seeing learners in uniform,
Huffing and puffing in our filthy central park
Thinking they have that spark . . .
Kore they even talk louder than bomme ba buang haholo kadi
taxing
Bare blofa ke the fun they had on Friday night . . .

Mothers and fathers trying to save their kids,
But all they say is "ke ja joy, ke ja botjha baka!"

At the end of the year they receive their reports
Otla a shapile smile seseng se kotsi . . .
Hare tla!
Repoto ere FAIL
Fail . . .

We would not put it past us

5 **2** *Len Verwey*

Call it a train, for like a train
it will take you away, to a secret children city
(call it a city) where you too might live
as you imagine princes live,
your bleakened faces radiant there.

Hahaha, but there can be no harm in waiting.
Keep your noses to the chill windowpane, wait
for that beam to sweep across you
some night much like this.

You want to ask us things, we know.
Where, for example, with the earth holed and cleft
and pilfered as it is, would the tracks be laid,
to keep a mass like that up?

You want to complain too, complain that if it runs
inside tunnels, deep beneath the ground,
one wouldn't hear its sound.
And there wouldn't be a beam.
And the station is an hour's walk away.

We understand what it is you're after.
You want to be reassured,
you think perhaps the game we play with you
was played with us too.

Maybe you are right: there is
a kind of vigil in us still, a gauntness

not so different from yours.
You are like us as we were before.
You are like us as we are now.
But if it is a game, the rules exclude
questions and complaints
and certain moves are not permitted.

We will not laugh to see you trample one another,
eager to get on, or wait until the last moment
then wrist-flick all that beautiful
machinery to hell and gone.

Pay attention though.
We would not put it past us to shake at you
after the fact, say listen,
there goes your train, you slept and missed it,
again, scab-kneed waiters, would-be princes,
snot-nosed hearkeners of nothing.

Come here, come stand with us instead.
Come and look at the morning.

Naguil

middernag (alweer) en my ore sing
seker om die geraas
van jou stem te onderdruk
ek moet jou uit my uit skryf
hierdie keer dig ek jou
(wat 'n meisie se vel
by die voordeur voorgekeer het)
    dood

jy wat in 'n wit kis gebore is
en seker so ook sal sterwe
waardig begrawe en waardig ontbind
twee dogters, een dogter, geen dogters later

en al wat van jou oor is
is 'n leë grafsteen
onder 'n dooie boom

Nocturnal

midnight (again) and my ears are ringing
probably to blot out
your raucous voice
I have to write you out of me
this time I'll pen you
(who barred a girl's skin
at the front door)
                    to death

you who were born in a white casket
and likely to die there
nobly buried and nobly decayed
two daughters, one daughter, no daughters later

and all that's left of you
an empty tombstone
under a dead tree

Versoeningsvers

wat weet jy
van getrou wees?

daar is die
vir wie tragedie
as geleentheid voorkom

ons is al nagenoeg
ses jaar
van mekaar geskei
deur geen hof
of grens
slegs my eie
nalatigheid

ek is gif

gister was ek te laat
ek het die blomme
op jou grafsteen
agtergelaat.

Reconciliation Verse

what do you know
of loyalty?

there are those
to whom tragedy
appears as opportunity

we are nearly
six years
divorced
through no court
or border
merely my own
negligence

I am poison

yesterday I was too late
I left the flowers
on your grave.

Fokof nou

hier binne
waar die lig in die hoeke opdam
bewe die mure
en my voete is vuil
en vuil en vuil en vuil

skree drie keer as ek jou
raak skryf; 'n gewone vers
is nie goed genoeg nie
: my ligamente is al moeg

hier binne (waar, binne)
stink dit na sweet
en 'n woede wat sidder
al langs ons verskuiwingslyn

ek meet my gemoed selfs nou
aan jou; 'n gebroke vers
wat my nie meer steur nie
: my ligamente is al rou

jy is gister
en ek en ek en ek
is vandag

Now Fuck Off

in here
where light piles up in the corners
the walls tremble
and my feet are foul
and foul and foul and foul

shout three times if I
make you write; a normal verse
isn't good enough
: my muscles have grown tired

in here (where, here)
it stinks of sweat
and a rage that shudders
all along our fault line

even now I measure my mood
by you; a broken verse
that doesn't plague me anymore
: my muscles have gone raw

you are yesterday
and I and I and I
am today

Lago

5 **4** *Mike Cope*

Arrived whiskers first
chewing this and that
among blown leaves
on a winter day
at a time of our need.
Someone we couldn't find
had abandoned him.
We took him in.

*

Small damp pink rubbery
tongue, accompanied by
light touch of whiskers
lick lick lick lick

*

We gave him names:
Ngubunny, Bunyata,
Walter Benjamin Bunny
Mr Boon, Doctor Rabbit,
and so on and more.
He knew our scent names
(which we don't.)

*

Exchanging body heat,
held in my arms
where my heart beat,
until the warmth
got through the clothes
and fur. He'd nuzzle in,
relax, lick any skin.

*

His greatest LEAP
clear
from the wardrobe,
four paces, six times his height
jack-in-a-box out of stillness
up onto the bed.

*

Loved Parrot Puffs
(fruit crackers for birds),
chocolate, raisins, dried fruit,
celery stalks, lettuce,
shoots from the avo tree.
Tolerated rabbit pellets.

*

Thumping, sometimes. Why?
Clicking claws on wooden boards.
A tiny cough or bark
his only word.
Displeasure.

*

Half-size (Netherlands dwarf),
he nipped the cats to make them preen,
pissed in my eye as he thundered by
in a firework circle on the bed,
scratch-scratch-scratched for a scrape on the rug,
ate the books, the clothes, the bag,
the shoes, the belt, the basket, the frame
of the door, gnawed at electric wires
and was generally a rascally rabbit
who taught us tidiness and vigilance.

A hundred and twenty moons he saw loop by,
serene in the black or through the windy clouds.
Nine times the avo tree took off its leaves
and budded flowers, and the bees were loud.
Three thousand three hundred nights he loped
inside to sniff about
and when the sun came out,
he came in, curious, as though he hoped
for novelty. Was I or the rabbit
the repetitive creature of habit?

*

Presents himself long and flat
to have the muscles beside his spine
massaged. Settles in for this.

*

Old, he no longer jumps
up to his chair for the sun.
Instead he lolls out flat,
a grey rag in a sunspot
on the floor.
At night I often see him
staring at the moon
or so it seems.
Perhaps he just craves light.

*

Guileless, un-envying
empty of hate, grudgeless,
without schemes or wiles.

*

Coat softer than granny's
fox-fur powder puff

*

Good night my old friend, I hope you sleep well,
My affection for you rings clear as a bell.
So often I have held your warm body to me,
Good night, little friend, sleep deep, dream free.

*

In the night by the rutted track,
crouching, a big hare
thinks he's a grey stone, a stone…
Four or five great leaps
into darkness. Gone
back to the eternal
pasturing of hares
on earth, among grasses.

The Rich, The Rich *(to be sung loudly)*

5 5 *Brent Meersman*

The rich, they shit on everything
in porcelain, china, marble bowl,
with toilet paper they use any thing.

The rich their arses clean bling-bling,
on the throne sit prone with toilet roll;
the rich, they shit on everything.

The rich make sure the stain won't cling,
with silk they wipe around the hole,
as toilet paper they use any thing.

The miners' safety, the poor's housing,
the tax return, the workers' payroll;
the rich, they shit on everything.

Christmas wrapping, bubble-wrap packing,
gemstones, people, mink or sable stole –
for toilet paper they use any thing.

When nature calls, the rich won't give a farthing
the melting pole, the global protocol.
The rich, they shit on everything;
for toilet paper they use any thing.

Does our ruin benefit the earth?

5 6 *Molefi Lebone*

"If I go first, I'll wait for you there,
On the other side of the dark waters," he told me.
"If I never meet you in this life, let me feel the lack.
A glance from your eyes and my life would be yours,"
I told him.

Minutes later I saw his charred body in the street.
Dancing, ululating and in shock, from standbys.
They just watched and stood back.
They had put a tyre around his neck
Till he became a running fire
Because he liked men.

He was my source of all that is going to be born.
He was my glory, my truth and my peace.

A father sjamboks his son.
To get rid of the filth,
He beats the demons out of him.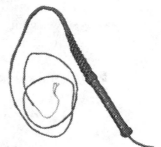
As he whips, he yells,
He is too soft.
He is too soft hearted.
He is not tough-fibred enough.

How did this evil steal into the world?
What seed, what root did it grow from?
What have we done to deserve this?
Why are they killing us,
Robbing us of life and light?
Does our ruin benefit the earth?
Does it help the grass to grow and the sun to shine?

My Lost Child

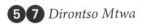 *Dirontso Mtwa*

I lost my child
When I asked questions
About my worth
And purpose for living

I lost my child
When my calling beckoned
And I followed my heart
And lived my dream

I lost my child
When I could not provide
Neither shelter for his head
Nor a plate on his table

I lost my child
Who stopped playing
Shutting himself out
All confidence lost

I lost my child
With his disrespect
He took control
Leading me to apathy

I lost my child
In crimes beyond belief
Violating my neighbour
Without even a blink

I lost my child
When discipline failed
He took me to court
Citing parental abuse

I lost my child
When I read the paper
He hung himself in shame
I buried him in despair

I lost my child
The day he was born
For I never knew
He was never mine

Boa Morte *(Song of Life)*

5 8 *Jana van Niekerk*

I remember you when you were young and vigorous

This is life
In the beginning
We all piss ourselves, it's not Austen

We wake up rumpled, we are bald
Our feet are hoary
The smell of haddock in the morning
The endless reshuffling of regrets and half-worn garments

This is not a place of fluffy handtowels
We are not brave all the time
The exhausting breakfast
The nauseating smell of chicken in the morning
The hard and predictable road back

It hurts like I am born

The animal afraid of losing himself
This cupboard of my tiny life
It is this simple, so

Tonight I just feel old

Death is always calling me
Be Aware
Write longer
I mourn myself,
My death, my passing, while I can

Life without Me
It hurts like I am born
You don't die easy, either
Surrender the fight

Either today tomorrow or later
We will hear the silence of our sleep
And I remember dying

Repeat: refrain, refrain
I mourn my passing
While I can

Yes, that too
Yes, all of that

And even our faces change

I remember you
breakfast smell in a hotel
this cupboard of my tiny life
I am Vivianne Westwood
I am Earnest Hemingway
It doesn't really matter
Though I sometimes think it does

Come back, come back

It's some way off but it's still there
The worms will eat this flesh
I do not love this flesh
I tie my fate to yours

By how much more can I make you mine
I tie myself to die

I dressed like an orphan
The light on the cupboard was like silver leaves
Silver rocks on the black mountain
I drank my milk
I washed my bum
Boa Morte: set down this
I am not dissatisfied

Ageing

There is a community of folk,
often invisible, overlooked
somewhat during busy days.

They move slowly, with ease,
making time seem insignificant
yet the morning's pre-eminent.

Neat, meticulous, hair groomed,
their style 's perfunctory,
carefully weather-conditioned.

Sometimes there's a hint of glamour:
an emphasized eyebrow, ruby lips,
blue-rinsed hair, spiffy cap.

Shopping is sound and sensible,
an odd small indulgence tossed in,
hesitantly.

There are signs that ankles hurt,
a nerve pinches, an eyelid sags,
copper bangles are a panacea.

Going home is about settling into orderliness,
where waiting is routine.
Memory a visitor.

Peace is paleness, a soft skin,
cup of tea and a light muffin,
stroking a cat in a scanty room

where the air is fresh,
light dim.

Love, mined

Love that is buried in a memory can be mined,
unearthed, brought to the surface,
raised towards the light,
and there be duly resurrected,
stroked, brushed, restored in shafts of the heart;
strung together ruby red,
glowing ceaselessly in eras
when mad men, mayhem, anarchic adventures,
hatred and greed,
shun love.

Between sediments of time,
love's cooled with tender songs, loyalty sublime,
yet stays undefiled,
intact and alive.

To revive such a love is to rebuke shadows,
defy age, the tyranny of time, foolish frailty;
love buried in memory is a rare find
yet a gift tied to time: sobering sorrows,
sombre days.

Inkanankana

Impilo ehalelwa izinkumbi,
Umkhosi ophithilizelisa abasha nezaguga,
Umkhosi odedelwa ulaxazwe njengomlilo,
Abawuphethe bayawuphihliza bebaleka,
Abawufunayo baphithizela njengamatsheketshe,
Umkhosi ozingelwa njengenyamazane.

Umkhosi omtoti ngamehlo,
Abawunambithayo bewuphimisa njengolwandle,
Abawubukayo bewulambele okwendodo,
Umkhosi owakhiwa eningini,
Kodwa othwala ngothando.

Umhlangano wezimpunzi ezimbili,
Unoxhaka obambela ukubulala,
Ungozi engapheli yasesiphongo,
Usuthombe siqoshwe ngensimbi.

Umkhosi oveza izithelo,
Izwe lakonhliziyo ngiyise,
Unkundla engavivinyelwa,
Umfundo eqheliselwa ingakafundelwa,

Unyango ngena wedwa,
Umvaleli wezimpelesi ngaphandle,
Ufindo eliqhaqhwa enkantolo liboshelwa ngaphandle,
Ufindo liboshwa nempelesi liqhaqhwa nabameli

Problem

Life yearned for by multitudes
A ceremony of the first fruits
That causes both young and old
To walk up and down
A ceremony looked down upon
Thrown away like fire
Those who carry fire destroy and run away
Those who want fire walk up and down like red ants
A ceremony hunted like wild animals
A ceremony of the first fruits attractive to the eyes
They taste and spit out like the sea
They look at and hunger for it like a medal
A ceremony harvested from multitudes
But who bare love

A gathering of two bulls
A trap that kills
A wound from the forehead that never heals
A sculpture crafted with steel

A ceremony that produces fruits
Land of the lost
Battlefield with no training
Education set aside before learning

The door where you enter alone
The door that locks bridesmaids outside
A knot unfastened in court and imprisoned outside
A knot imprisoned with a bridesmaid
Set free by the lawyers

Translation by Siphiwe ka Ngwenya

Isizukulwane

Ondlebe kazizwa abaphikelela kwagoqanyawo
Osehla senyuka njengamatsheketshe
Bephithizelisa okwezibonkolo
Beklama beqatha angalinywayo
Bephihliza ezekhethelo lempilo

Bekhalakathela njengezimvu emgedeni
Bephuphutheka njengezimvukuzane emhlabathini
Bengqengqemuka ngohleko lokufa
Begigitheka ngisho seligeqwa
Isizukulwane sasendle

Onontanda kubukwa
Abaphilisa okwezitibane
Abagadlwa ngenduku eyodwa bephindelelwa
Begqimuzwa bedekezwa ezingeqiwa ntwala
Isizukulwane sokweduka

Onkani yakhe omphikeleli
Abanhlanhlatha ngisho beyibona inyathuko
Bephulukundlela okwesikhukhula sikadomoyi
Bephoqoza amafa abo okwesiphepho
Begugula izimpilo zabo okwezikhukhula
Isizukulwane sokulahlwa

Onokuzula abajigimisa okonogwaja
Beqansa izintaba ezingaqanswa
Bephila eyokugigitheka neyokuzilawuya
Beyizimpunzi zasendle uqobo
Maluju azibuye emasisweni

The Past

What were you thinking, mother,
When you handed me the slim rectangular package –
A watch for my tenth birthday –
When I came to your bed that lonely winter morning?

I was mute with my longing for your love;
You, a distant angel, in buttoned-up Victorian nighty,
Dim morning light yellowing the pulled blind.

The quiet of that first house echoes in me now;
The time between an empty ache.
Later that day you would listen to Mahler's *Songs of the Earth,*
Music heavy as a bowl of stones resting on a table;
Covering the record sleeve, Monet's field of crimson poppies –
My father's first gift of music to you.

In the deep recesses of memory, you and I lodge,
The years billowing back like soft muslin curtains
To show the garden of the soul,
The verdant tree of childhood still standing,
The flagstones of my person laid down, flooring me.

Winter Braai

The stubby fingers of a bare frangipani
Scrabble toward scraps of night cloud
As a small wind blows at the bulwark of the house
Like a tired child might push against her immovable mother.

One bright star stares from an insistent blackness –
A silent omniscient eye –
As closer to earth
The moving air whispers: look, look,
Look again, and listen.

The leaves want you to hear their rustle,
While the small white frog that you threw from your hands
Into the undergrowth, has landed, unharmed,
And chirrups: a counterpoint to the crickets.

There are seeds nubbing even in this wintry ground;
So close to and part of the dark.
They are another summer's skeleton.

On the verandah you sit next to a black cauldron
That cradles its red fire –
An effulgence of heat –
Flames springing up to harden the soft bodies of hake
Doused in olive oil and lemon,
Laid out on the grid.

You sip the cold air
As if it might offer solace, like whisky;
Your family indoors and the evening fanning out around you
Lonely as palm fronds arcing from one trunk –
Thick, separate stripes,
Awkward against a dull orange sky.

The storm, Krotoa's ally

I am the storm, I am the
sea's reflection, it's other self
I watch as (in these rough
natal days) this little child is swept up
as dust with a broom
trod on, as the mud & grass
at your fort

This is krotoa's world
why is it so streaked with shadows
why is it so laden with cracked leaves,
exploding patterns, ripples of shadows
in the golden light

on many nights I wash up
mighty waves against your shores
seeking to agitate your dreams
trying to seed a new song &
a new warmth in your veins

this child who can interpret my moods
who reads the plants
deciphers the grunts and glares of men –
in your grinding words & downward gaze
are you trying to break our spirit?

now what is left?

the futility of broken bracelets; of
khoi clothes torn off her
and replaced with garments of
the 'company'
and what will you learn?

I, the tempest; the swirling belly
of the cloud
I churn your dreams
when you puff up, cramp your gut
I rouse long buried truth from embers
I burn a light though your bones

even down the ages

This hand

these fingers broken in many parts –
knuckled, buckled
as i try to give
a segment
to so much that needs so much
to plug gaps, broken fences
small cracks in dreams

this hand broken (or sprained
temporarily lame or momentarily inflamed)
by pen, by welding machine, by hammer or
drenched in turpentine
as i sought for bread
to fill this hollow, this basic need
hardened & coarsened
by these times, these truths

this black hand —once no clasping with white
now: shaking in peace
& what of all that's been lost
in the fire
what of singed hair, smoke-stained skin,
streaked eyes

we turn those into memories
that sit snugly or roughly
in a patterned frame

the arts

a lightning rod for love
a weather vane
of pain
a cairn for the dying, headstone for the dead
a walking stick
for the stony winding road
that circles us

a stick to taunt the beast
a question
going up in flames
a mat on which
my widowed soul
mourns the shattered trust

in my palm
the broken compass
to keep me seeking
to keep me forest-wandering
until i hear the talking tree &
scratch the soothing cactus

Thirst

I lived in a land of drought
stark, harsh

do not smuggle your stepmother's shampoo
her hair is lush with water
and your father's love
her skin - never scrubbed
she grows roses
pretty, greedy and foreign

you are small, untidy, tough
a boer
you belong to broken lands like this one.

Sea Shells

I gather seashells like men
make a pretty necklace out of them

mussels
cavalier, cutting, chaotic

I gather seashells with men
wear colour when I write

whelks
timid, taut, territorial

I gather seashells as men
seek souls

perlemoen
gleaming, guileless. Godly.

National University Shutdown, South Africa, October 2015

My lover

there was a day like yours once –
the first of a year, with gin and dry lemon, on a green garden patio, when I
still ate potatoes
how hungry I was
to live/love/learn
I didn't know, then –

Blue dye on voluptuous knees.
A grandmother looks away while a grandson is thrown.
Shopping for nappies for children chased from their homes (and cigarettes
for their mothers).
Thank-full when the priests came – surely they will not hate us now?
Tearing blackface posters down, trying to breathe through my breasts.
My voice crawling down my throat to hide in my gut.
Vomiting wheels – my body a small child begging, "Please don't make me."
"I'm sorry Granny. I can't defend your faith here. They will lynch me."

Characters in a Psychologist's Waiting Room

1. the Girl with eyes wider than her thighs
2. the Boy who keeps his face covered in the hallways – always
3. the Woman who sleeps beneath the purple blanket she
    brings in her bag
4. there are no men.

Trade Winds *(An extract from "Vespa Diaries')*

6 **4** *Ari Sitas*

Hard winter this

I'll lend you a 300mm lens for your click-clack he said,
only if you fetch me fresh snoek for the braai!
Fair trade
harsh trade winds,
low clouds

Climbing the mount to reach Kalk Bay harbour
through the sheets of rain
wind-lashing rain
after trucking past hundreds of Khwe ghosts panting up and up
the uphill
singing in an unapproved language
then past the hundreds of Khwe ghosts panting down and down
the downhill
singing something quite obviously subversive,
to face the furious surf
to breathe-in the seepage of kelp
to point out the prized dead snoek

Hard town this town
"No fish today", the sea cracks timber cracks spines
drowns men
I have some snoek in the freezer at Nordhoek
says the fisherman
quite dead and ready

Relax have some of this sweet gut-love

3 litres past the fourth box of Autumn Harvest
life gets philosophical:

"There is no synagogue by Silver Mine"
"There was no silver in the mine to justify such
inglorious deaths"

Wrapped fish somewhere in Nordhoek
in three layers of Malema newsprint
to thaw
and when it thawed
Malema helped to quarantine the stench
and dreamt of the lens and the baobab highways
of the north
where the lion roams
not just the hapless penguin

There has to be a place for us –
between the fable and the fact
perhaps, Macondo again
quite unexplored, somewhere far
past the cracked busts of leaders
in an uncommissioned space
a space of birds, yes, loud birds
even if their tenor shrieks unsettle dawn
where even fixing a mosquito net tight is an act of love

because this country hurts.

                    *

A Vespa?
I happen to belong to a community that never tires of testing my
limits, of trivialising my quests.
A Vespa!- laughter, guffaws – Get the man a drink!-
You will never get the girl! Give it up!!!
OK: I agree that Vespas are what ducks are to the civilisation of birds.
More of a wader than falcon, cruisers rather than speedsters but you
must agree they are substantial enough not to be confused for speed-
bumps by suburban 4X4s.

They are about solidity and balance.
As long as the fierce winds are tail-winds
They do allow their rider a sense of the panorama!
Get real.
A sense of what we could be sharing as a vision.
OK Bishop Tutu take a seat . . .
Zen and the art of motorcycle countenance.
And a freedom to yank the goggles off . . . and you can see properly
because the speed that insects fly into your eye does not allow
the critters to split your retina.
It is also an anti-imperialist gesture: brings with it less of the American
counter-culture and the jingoism of Easy Rider but the cultural finesse
of the 1960s Italian black and white movies whose directors' names-
apart from Fellini - escape me.
He will write his Vespa Diaries, how pretentious is that!?
Fellini meets Van der Post!
He wants a woman!
Che in Doornfontein!
I would only do it on a donkey…
A donkey cart…
No, with a rickshaw-wallah pulling.
Yes, and with a swarm of butterflies forming a halo over the trudging
cart . . . pure Rusdhie . . . pure post-modern Bollywood.
No, with a cart, with donkeys and a grand piano on wheels behind . . .
No, walking . . . with a rucksack filled with peanut butter, Bovril,
cheese and crackers and an apple your lover kissed into the sack to give
you melancholia.
Eat this morons: according to Umberto Eco and Omar Calabrese in
their book Cult of Vespa . . .
Umberto Eco?
Umberto Eco, yes – untold numbers of Fakirs in Cantadore outfits
strumming guitars enter the room. I have my wits' total attention.
Umberto Eco!
There are roses, seduction, a sense of some quiet grandeur.
I dropped a name!
Umberto Eco, yes. A whole book on the Vespa!

A semiotic coup-d'etat!
Shut up!
A Vespa?
Not a Vuka?
No, a Vespa.

May the lines on the road keep firm so you do not slip and crack a metaphor.
May the trucks take notice of you.
May drunken and cell-phone chatting teenagers give you some respite.
May dogs respect your pantaloons.
May the badass Kudu not leap into your path at night.
And may the leopard walk off your camp fire.
Come on, be a troo man.

*

Do troo men ever rhyme?
Ngidal'umlilo:
Troo men don't rhyme
Troo men don't swank
They just climb up verses
They crank up the stanzas almost iambic
Their rhythms are lean, their heartbeat lank
Their rhythms are lean and when in trouble…lank
Ngidal'umlilo- taram aram
I also suppose
Troo women don't scowl
They scoff at the brinjal
Etcetera

Anywhere

Be there.
Being there.
Meaning much.
And nothing.

I'll be there.
There for you.
I'm here.
Where is here?

Am I there?
Where are you?
Not with me. Not here.
So where?
Not here.
Maybe there.

But not here.

Because

Not:

Because I love you.
Because you tempt me.
Because you stole me.
Because I promised.
Because you saw.
And I knew you watched.

And then you lied.

But
Because you comfort me.
Because you hide me.
And you assure me.
Every day I'm asking:

Is why I stay.

The Man Who Wished He was Lego

His hands would be yellow
and forever curved
into a semi-square "C."
Designed only for quick
and easy snapping

of pieces meant
to fit. His shoes
would be the same colour
as his pants with no zips
or buttons, no pockets

for slipping in notes
that could be shredded
in the wash. He would need
not worry about the shape
of his head, or haircuts

and thoughts for that matter.
And best of all, his chest
would be stiff and hollow,
far too small
for a heart.

The Basket and the Road

(after a photograph by Mimo Khair of an unknown farmer)

Perhaps you will wash the dust trapped
in the folds of your skin with precious water
later. Not before you have unloaded what you hope
to sell: bright yellow squash in a basket
full to the brim they could tumble out

should you miss an uphill step. Straps
of flattened rope cut into your shoulders
like tire trucks on mud. But no one
can see them under your shirt.
Strands of what looks like a horse's tail

hang between you and the woven
basket falling the length of your torso.
What I see from your eyes matters
little to you. Another pebble
shaken free between your toes

on a misty Yunnan morning.
The road ahead of you and behind
changes only with the seasons.
What you bear I can only imagine,
comfortable as I am

that it isn't mine even
for a moment. I can stare
as long as I want and you will still
be there, right foot completing
a step while left heel beginning to lift.

How to Make a Salagubang Helicopter

They prefer mango trees, but any tree
will have at least one. A quick shake
and they fall like pebbles, these beetles.
Some still in the act of mating, they glisten
with droplets of monsoon rain.

One of the bigger boys told me
their prickly legs are harmless,
like thin petals of a flower
opening and closing. "Here,"
he said, handing me one

in the hollow of his fist.
On the lines of my palm,
this salagubang couldn't push
itself upright with the stiff
covers of its wings.

He picked up another beetle,
held it close to my face
and placed index and middle
finger on the grooves of its body.
With the other hand he snapped

off the two kicking back legs.
On their stumps he tied
a thread and on it, with the span
of a hand, knotted a stone.
The salagubang flew

when he let it go,
but only in circles with the stone
dead center. We laughed.
I could feel the wind
from frantic wings.
How I started writing on a notepad

How I started writing on a notepad

I got to write on a notepad because nako tse kaofela, ke ntse ke sa ngoale mo notepadding, you know, I used to write poetry on random pieces of paper, o kile wa bona, just here and there. And before I get to that other part ya di "amen" and all that stuff, from the first poems I used to write. But how I got to write on a notepad, actually, was very interesting, because what happened? I was in my father's car, and my mother had just got the car from my father, coz at the time this was after my accident, and ko skolong they were talking about "yho! Ngoana o na re tlo mo koba" ntho tse joalo, "ha e beng a ka tla late futhi" because at that time I was in a wheelchair, you know, so, ok hold on…alright sho, hola. And then so now, so ba re ngoana o re tlo mo koba ntho tse joalo, ha a ka tla late futhi, o kile wa bona, and my mother was going mad, because my father had a car at the time, and, and, modimo, e thata taba e.

So joanong, my mother decides to get the car, and ha a gutla ka transi, she takes me to school in my father's car, and I felt so proud, like oh shit, ok, ke vaya ka transi ya le thaima, yho! go monate di ya boya, ok, and at the time my father used to drive a BMW, hahahah, 318, o a e bona ntho e joalo. So, and an automatic too but regardless. So ha ntse re vaya re ya ko s'ghela, oh sorry, sho, beer e go a nyewa.

Anyway. So ha ntse re vaya re ya ko s'ghela, eerrm, I look inside the glove compartment, you know, ha ke re, I find my father's notepad, o wa ngoala daar, he's got his poetry, you know, sho! one more time, sorry, Black Label what you doing. So oa ngoala daar, entlek o ngoetse, he has written most of his poems on a notepad and I read it and I read it, and the first one I come across, ke daai ding e a e ngoetseng ka Africa, a poem about Africa or something like that, and this is how I literally start writing on a notepad, and I am like oh wow, if my father is doing the same thing, I might as well do the same thing, because to me my father was like my hero jo, you know, he was like the ultimate god, e ne e le motho o ha ke mo shebile, ke bona he's never laid a hand on me or my brother, he's never laid a hand on Sthu and me, whatsoever.

Maara. I was afraid of him, it's a kind of fear that was of respect, because everybody respected him for who he was apart from what he did, a very strong headed man, very together person, o ka tla re mo lala wa gage ha o gone go thikazisega, ntho tse joalo, you know, so now, I get to school in my father's car, great stuff, beautiful, fantastic, the morning was like any other morning, and thankfully azange ka fitlha late ko skolong, coz my mother had been stressing, you know KES, eish, anyway, KES e na le matlakala sometimes but it's understandable it's a school that is running on its own semi private kind of rules, you know. So, granted, if your child comes to school late again, you guys, you in shit, and given the fact ya gore I went to that school under extreme conditions, because the MEC of education at the time was Mary Metcalfe she told them go re no no o a tseba keng, "here is a boy in a wheelchair who is going to come and if you guys don't allow him to come to your school we going to put your educational board under review", ntho tse joalo, you know, and I am thinking, oh great stuff, and my mother has been working left right and centre to keep me in school, and I've been going up and down ka dicombi, you know, transport was not being right, and the time my mother didn't have a car, ok great, this is the first year, the first year as in '97, first year high-school, at the time I was still in a wheelchair, and I mean you don't have a lot of options when you're in a wheelchair, coming from the township going to a school in the suburb, you don't have much option, but my mother hustled to get me into the school, great, lovely.

Now, on this particular day, eer, now, I get to school in my father's car, my mother drops me off and, sho, ok, my mother drops me off e be a tsamaya, it was like any other normal school day jo, you know, went through the old routine, five past eight skolo sa qala and then, you know, I mean ke skolo jo, so come five past two, or ten past two ba tlo nlata joanong, hao! Ke latiwa ke maolady le mamogolo S'bongile. Mamogolo S'bongile le maolady? What's going on here? But anyway, mamgol S'bongile is my godmother, and this is my mother's closest friend you know, so, ba nlata mo le ka koloi, and ra vaya, but what I hear has been happening while I was in school, yho! It becomes even more hectic, and after so many years this is what I have heard, and I have been told, what happened tsatsi le le. Apparently that morning, when my mother went to go get the car ko le thaima, let me have a cigarette, well when that happens. Uuuhhm, my mother went there a tsamaya le Tebza, well, I'll give a character break down ya Tebza.

Tebza jo, is one person, o e leng sextsharo, a good looking brother, my late uncle was a very good looking brother, man, shit, you know, and I mean ladies loved that man, he was like the most harmless person, the most non violent person you know, but I suppose growing up in the township, you're exposed to violence so much that you become violent without realising that you are violent, hahaha, anyway, aothi e na ke konyana, Tebza is like the guy who jokes a lot. So, my mother gets to the house, at the time I was living with my mother, and by then they had been separated for some time but and it was crunch time now, if I don't get to school early, I get kicked out, so o a kokota o a kokota o a kokota, eyi, ha kokota, my father comes down, this is the house that, everything had sort of broke down to a certain degree, di ntho tse ngata di le di a senyega daar, you know, I mean that was literally the first time I ever heard my mother scream, I have seen shit like that, that house was cursed but let me not blame the building, hahaha, you know, it's just a cop out thing, you know, it's art love supreme after all. So now, le thaima li le la bula monyako daar, la re, "What you guys doing here, what's up", and my mother tells him, "Maakomele o ba tla koloi, he needs transport to go to school man" and my father is like, "Nah, I can't give you the car". And I think him saying no sort of triggered violence in my uncle, in this sextsharo sweet handsome good looking man, o a e bona ntho eo?

Atmosphere e vetse ya changer completely, and as soon as my father said "No, I can't give you my car to take my own son to school", this guy, this slender looking brother, who was actually not even bigger than my father, pushed down the door, a beya le thaima mo le siting, and my mother walked in, like an enraged bull, she charged in more than walked in. A kena a lata di khiya, this I am told, and I can only imagine how it was because of the tone my mother was telling me in, from what I could hear from her telling me, I could only imagine how she got in to that house, you know, she didn't walk in she charged in, ke le wa bona, like an elephant on heat, like she didn't care, like, "A ke kgathale go tseba now, I am going to get the keys, my son needs to go to school". Err fuck, so my mother gets the keys, and then, she storms out with the car, while my uncle has this man, my father, on lockdown, like "Hei, you not doing anything, you not going nowhere", you know, "we taking your son to school mathafaka what tha fuck!" set-up you know. So ba tswe ka koloi, bbbrrrrrr, ke bale ba tswa, and my mother says she almost hit a car. She was not completely telling me all of this, she was telling mamogolo S'bongile in the car. I am gathering all of this from in the car, from school going back home, you know, so my mind is racing, pacing, and I am putting all this shit together. Apparently, eeerr, before ba nka koloi ko ntlong, my father says to her, "ha o ka nka koloi e na, ke tlo go tshoarisa, I am taking you to the police, man", sho! and I think, that also e le e a qah qah fuse to the fullest in my uncle's head, they stormed out with the car, she almost hit something, came to pick me up, and this I didn't know, and I didn't know any of this my mother being my mother, hahha, she comes cool calm and collected, and I didn't see nothing of that sort, ha ke re, wow, "so le thaima le go file koloi?" a re "ya" you know, and she is like that, even now she is like that, she won't tell you, go re ya no, there is something wrong at home, blah blah blah. So sho, cigarette. Now, eerr, apparently, actually I am told, not even apparently, I am told, that, ha ntse ke le ko skolong, my father did actually do what he said he was going to do, and called the police and reported the car stolen, my god, "by whom", the police say to him and he says, by his wife, oh my god. "Why?" he doesn't say. You know, he doesn't say why the car was stolen by his wife, so ba tla ko gae ko Zone 6, with my aunts, but I am not sure maara my father's older sister, was the one o a na di gatela ko pele, who was on some "ya vele, you must do this, wara wara wara wara" bullshit.

She kept going on, a re "tshoanetse le mo tshoare, he he he he" you know, and they were all behind my father, but that was sort of ashamed, was my grandfather, the person I am named after, e a nko tloisa bo tloko taba e, it's sad. When the police came and took her from home, to the police station, I mean there is a case against my mother for theft, for stealing a car, you know, so ha fetla ko stashining, ba motsa, "go e tsa getseng daar" and she says "no, ke e nkile koloi, from my husband" "why?" "ne ke batla go tsamaisa ngoanaka ko skolong, ngoanaka o so le so le so, o gobetse, o tsamaya ka wheelchair, blah blah blah" at least I would think that's what she said, you know, and the police were like, "mxha, my sister, eish le authi yakho, i yenza kanjani, yazi le authi yakho, eish" you know, and after I heard that, my love for my name died completely, well from where my name comes from, I have always been my name, but it died completely, but one thing I remember ultimately, I remember today from that day is why I write on a notepad, remembering how it all happened ahh fuck it's hectic.

So that's how I start writing on a notepad,
so every time I write, it's as if I go back there again.

The Silence of Words

        i am sorry Mama
i cannot tell you
      what you want to hear
i can see
           my fear in your eyes
your tongue like my heart
cannot hold the words
              that steal
                my breath
i am trying Mama
sometimes I lose myself
        to question marks
      that ask:
"whose blood will carry this line?"
           i am sorry Mama
some words cannot outrun reality
       they do not allow us
to exhale
         what we want to say

Take Away

take away
the pot of now
this rainbow
is empty

what will I feed
my unborn words
when this diseased cold
pages over old bones?
tonight, the spirit ink and I dance
the *Mokama* dance
so take away the pain
in waiting
that sleepless fight
when nameless cows
burn suns
from their father's eyebrows

take away that speechless plight
between a woman's thighs
when her barren gates
search for something
other than this "light"

take away everything
everything that takes me away
away from staying
staying away from everything
that passes away

but please!
don't take me away
from my sacrament
when Malombo is on
unplugging the rainbow
from this unstable pot

Sunday drive in the Overberg

6 8 *Heidi Grunebaum*

To the top of Franschoek pass
we drive and on to the Overberg:
Villiersdorp and Grabouw.
Only silence speaks through the broken landscape
through quilted miles of its velvet blossom promise,
apples, peaches, apricots, plums.
Until fields greet aching azure mountains,
early twilight shadows casting purple rays
over waterfalls as they silver towards mountain pools.
There the earth's beauty shrinks,
shiny Landrovers whizz through dust and denial
towards nostalgic architecture,
Cape Dutch homesteads.

We pass by sardine-can reserves,
backyards of human life called "labour"
by those whose power to name mutes from history
the late-night hands that work the land;
the moon-filled songs of sadness, wine-soaked longings.
Ever-walking legs trudge with water, fire-wood,
tired women, children too small to walk,
bearing memories too sore to speak
and dreams and chattels strapped
to the enduring backs of ancestors:
chained to these patchwork acres, an endless death
whose harvest profits the shameless hunger
of white Wabenzis and captured treats.

Through history, tarred over by the highway,
we drive back towards the obliterating city.
Dunes of unmoored sand roll by,
this emasculated land unseeded of hope

or the promise of orchards, heavy and ripe
or lazy Sunday strolls; past flickering, zinc-chained shacks –
here board, there cement – this 'development',
"poverty reduction" by those whose power to name
keeps stolen profits in new and old pockets;
until finally the great mountain, immaculate sentinel,
rises up from the misty rays of the last day's sun.

Poems and Persecution in Occupied Palestine:
The Trial of *Dareen Tatour*

This feature looks at the way the Israeli state attacks artists who dare raise issues of national and individual oppression in Occupied Palestine.

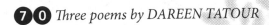 *Three poems by DAREEN TATOUR*

I'll Forget It, As You Wish
Translated Jonathan Wright

As you wish,
I'll forget it,
The story of us that's now part of the past
And the dreams that were once the fill of our hearts.
We would have liked to make them come true,
But we killed them.
I'll forget things, o love of my life,
Things we said,
The poems we wrote on the walls of our hearts
And drew in colors,
The trees under which we sat for a time,
And the names we carved.
I'll forget them,
As you wish,
So don't be angry.

I Will Not Leave
Translated by Jonathan Wright

They signed on my behalf
And turned me into
A file, forgotten
Like cigarette butts.
Homesickness tore me apart
And in my own country I ended up
An immigrant.
I abandoned those pens
To weep over the sorrows
Of the inkwells.
They abandoned my cause and my dream
At the cemetery gates
And that person who's waiting
Laments his luck
As life passes.
Besiege me,
Kill me, blow me up,
Assassinate me, imprison me.
When it comes to my country,
There's no backing down.

Resist, My People, Resist Them

Resist, my people, resist them.
In Jerusalem, I dressed my wounds and breathed my sorrows
And carried the soul in my palm
For an Arab Palestine.
I will not succumb to the "peaceful solution,"
Never lower my flags
Until I evict them from my land.
I cast them aside for a coming time.
Resist, my people, resist them.
Resist the settler's robbery
And follow the caravan of martyrs.
Shred the disgraceful constitution
Which imposed degradation and humiliation
And deterred us from restoring justice.
They burned blameless children;
As for Hadil, they sniped her in public,
Killed her in broad daylight.
Resist, my people, resist them.
Resist the colonialist's onslaught.
Pay no mind to his agents among us
Who chain us with the peaceful illusion.
Do not fear doubtful tongues;
The truth in your heart is stronger,
As long as you resist in a land
That has lived through raids and victory.
So Ali called from his grave:
Resist, my rebellious people.
Write me as prose on the agarwood;
My remains have you as a response.
Resist, my people, resist them.
Resist, my people, resist them.

The Arrest of Dareen Tatour
Revital Hovel

Dareen Tatour, 35, of Reineh in northern Israel, was charged in November 2015 with incitement to violence and support for a terror organization because of three items she posted on Facebook and YouTube. According to the indictment, one video shows masked men throwing rocks and Molotov cocktails at Israeli forces. In the background, Tatour is heard reading her poem (printed above) whose English title is *"Resist, my people, resist them."*

The day after uploading the video, she wrote in a post: "The Islamic Jihad movement hereby declares the continuation of the intifada throughout the West Bank. ... Continuation means expansion ... which means all of Palestine. ... And we must begin within the Green Line ...for the victory of Al-Aqsa, and we shall declare a general intifada. #Resist." The State Prosecutor's Office interpreted this text as support for Islamic Jihad and a new intifada.

The third allegedly criminal post was uploaded five days later. It was a photograph of Asra'a Abed, a 30-year-old Israeli Arab woman who was shot and wounded by police after waving a knife at officers in the bus station in Afula in October 2015. Tatour captioned the image, "I am the next shahid," or martyr.

Two days later the police arrested Tatour at her home. In her request to hold Tatour for the duration of legal proceedings, prosecutor Alina Hardak cited the "real danger to public welfare" posed by her posts.

After initially denying any connection to the Facebook page and the image of Abed, Tatour told investigators that, like other Arab poets, she writes about prisoners and her homeland. She stressed that her intentions were nonviolent, that she doesn't want to be a shahida and that she favors only peaceful means.

In January 2016 Tatour was released, after being fitted with an ankle monitor, to house arrest at the home of her brother in Kiryat Ono, which has no internet access. After successive relaxations of the terms of her house arrest, Tatour holds down a part-time retail job, but is still prohibited from accessing the internet. A verdict is expected soon.

*   *   *

The Jewish State versus Dareen Tatour
Yehuda Shenhav

Dareen Tatour is a Palestinian citizen of Israel who lives in the village of Reineh near Nazareth. She had dreamed of being a poet since she was a child. Alina Hardak, the diligent and determined Israeli prosecutor, destroyed her dream by attempting to prove that Tatour is not a real poet. This came to light in public, in an unprecedented ars-poetic theatrical hearing held at the courthouse.

The prosecutor, who can be imagined wearing a cloak and brandishing a sword, insists for seven full hours on resolving the irresolvable riddle of poetry, namely, who is a poet? As if it was the poetic equivalent of Fermat's Last Theorem.

The prosecutor is an attorney. She has a career and is trying to be objective, as her profession demands. But she also has thoughts, and once in a while the mouth releases what those thoughts are. You must read it to believe it. Instead of the hearing discussing the semantic and political implications of a poem written in Arabic for Arabs, the hearing in the palace of justice revolves around the "credibility" of its translation into Hebrew.

I was not in the courtroom myself, but here are a few of the things that were said there, which together make up a theater of the absurd of two systems.

Act One: Who is a poet?

Witness: Prof. Nissim Calderon, who teaches Hebrew poetry and edits a poetry journal.
Cross examination: About two hours
Prosecutor: You begin by assuming the accused is a poet.

W: Yes.
P: You agree that you have no prior acquaintance.
W: I read the indictment, and there's a poem there, and the person who wrote the poem is a poet.
P: Who defines a poem?
W: There is no authoritative entity. ... What the poet defines as a poem is a poem.
P: How do you know the poet defines it as a poem?
W: It was published in short lines, and when it has a rhythmic element we can reasonably assume it's a poem. ... "Resist, resist my people," that's musicality that stems from repetition. There's a musical and literal connection in the refrain ... The prosecutor also understood that it's a poem.
P: If I write a text eight lines long, and after every two lines, two lines are repeated, is that a poem to you?
W: Yes.

The prosecutor delves into the differences between prose, poetry, a figure of speech, reliable poetry and imitative poetry. She apparently disagrees with generations of giants. Tatour is not a poet, even if this isn't her first poem in Arabic and contains a rhythmic element and short lines that repeat. If she is a poet, the trial is a farce; in a democracy, poets are not tried and cut off from the world for a year and a half.

In a democracy, poetry enjoys creative freedom, minority opinions must be heard, etc. The prosecutor won't allow Tatour to be called a poet, because if she is a poet, Israel is China or North Korea.

The prosecutor begins to realize that she is arguing with a leftist academic. She tenses when the expert explains that the poem was written in a genre customary to Palestinian national poetry, that there are thousands like it and they have parallels in all national poetry traditions, including Zionism.

When the witness says there is no authority to determine what is a poem, the prosecutor resolves to prove that the court is hearing a leftist disguised as an objective witness.

She cites an event the witness took part in, "Poetry in the Shadow of Terror," in Tel Aviv.

We can only assume that the prosecutor will demand regulations and a code of ethics for poets. The Culture Ministry will establish a licensing unit for poets, with rules against poetic negligence. The Public Security Ministry will guard against impersonators, who may be jailed without charges. The Health Ministry will revoke the license of a poet who has suffered an attack of lunacy or divine inspiration (whichever comes first).

Now the indefatigable prosecutor must prove that "shahid" means terrorist. She asks her translator to take the stand.

The witness is an old man, with 30 years in the Nazareth police. For the first time in his life, he is being asked to translate a literary text into Hebrew.

When his translation was submitted to the court, he apologized for flaws and omissions. Much was lost in translation. And "shahid"? He got stuck in the middle, between Arabic and Hebrew. "Shahid" is "shahid." For the prosecution that's enough, because in Hebrew culture a shahid is a terrorist.

But the next witness, an expert on translation for the defense, enumerates various dictionary definitions of shahid: a martyr, one who has fallen in battle, a victim." I assume the prosecutor realized that once again she had before her a witness who is not objective and has leftist views. Apparently it's important that every word in Arabic have only one meaning in Hebrew, even if it's removed from its semantic context. For the prosecution, it was preferable to leave shahid in Hebrew transliteration, and to rely on its meaning in Hebrew culture — as though a word in Arabic and the meaning with which it was burdened in Hebrew are identical.

Act Two: Who is a translator?
The witness: Dr. Yonatan Mendel, a translator and researcher of Hebrew-Arabic translation. Cross examination: about five hours.

In the cross examination, during which it seemed that the witness had become the accused, short films (unrelated to Dareen Tatour), were screened that showed scenes of rioting all over the West Bank. The soundtrack repeatedly voiced words such as "shahids," "terror," "blood," "the sanctity of the land" and "the right of return," until to Jewish ears it seemed as though these were quotes from the poems of Uri Zvi Greenberg we studied in class: "Blood will determine who will be the sole ruler"; "A land is conquered with blood. and only when conquered with blood is hallowed to the people with the holiness of the blood"; "A return to the village is a miraculous return, the felled tree returns to connect to its source"; "I hate the peace of those who surrender."

P: Do you consider yourself an objective witness?
W: Yes.
P: How good is your knowledge of Arabic?
W: It's excellent.
P: When you're listening, it's hard for you to understand. Why?
W: There's a difference between simultaneous interpretation and translation of a written document.

P: In your opinion, is the Palestinian people a people living under occupation?

W: The Palestinian people are a divided people, they don't live in a free country.

P: Do you think that there's a right to resist the occupation?

W: I'm in favor of nonviolent resistance.

P: Now you claim Israelis automatically interpret "shahid" as related to terror.

W: Correct.

P: You say the Israeli-Jewish interpretation of the word is really distorted ... and every Palestinian who hears it understands it as "those who have fallen" and not as "shahids"?

W: I would say more as "victims," not as "aggressors."

P: Previously your wrote "those who have fallen" as opposed to "shahids," and now you're saying "victims" as opposed to "aggressors."

W: The word shahids — in Hebrew it's fraught, the vast majority of the shuhadaa, or in Hebrew "shahids," are civilians who didn't go out to harm Israelis.

P: In the police translation it sounds like a call for violence. You translated "one who rises up," whereas he translated "one who resists."

W: The root of the word in Arabic is kuf-yud-mem — and I'm looking for a similar root in Hebrew, "rose up." " "Resisted" is not a mistake, but "rose up" is more appropriate.

Maybe someone will also propose the "Translation Law," since it's impossible for a specific word to have several translations.

And that's how the discussion of a poem in Arabic is conducted in Hebrew, by people who don't have a sufficient concept of Arabic. Equipped with a Robinson Crusoe mentality, they are certain that Friday will speak their language, and believe that every word in a language that they don't understand has only one meaning in Hebrew. All the more so, when it comes to a familiar word like "shahid."

The long hours that the court spent surrounding the issue of the translation are a masquerade, trickery. Does anyone really think that such a discussion can be conducted in Hebrew? The translation came up because the prosecutor — like everyone else in the courtroom   doesn't understand Arabic. Because if the discussion had been conducted in Arabic, an official language in Israel, the court wouldn't have needed a translator. We would expect a prosecuting body with integrity, which time after tme repeated the presumption of objectivity, to bow its head and to set aside the case.

But the prosecution also knew about a 2015 study that found that only 0.4 percent of Israeli Jews are capable of understanding a complex text in Arabic. For its own reasons, the prosecution did not set aside the case. On the contrary, its determination to assemble a cast for the theater of the absurd only increased.

P: [The poem] is not referring only to the West Bank.
W: Correct.
P: And actually there's also a reference here to within the
      Green Line.

Like a shot in a concert hall, the Green Line is the issue. That's the unfortunate boundary line that has long since been erased from the Jews' maps, in an impressive colonialist process. Nobody talks about the Green Line any more except for our prosecutor, the anti-Semites at the United Nations and a handful of peace envoys who visit the region from time to time. The Jews no longer have a Green Line, Yesha (Judea and Samaria) is here, and this is the land of our forefathers, and the Jews cross the Green Line, but only the Jews. And so that the Palestinians — in other words those who are called Israeli Arabs - don't cross the Green Line, it has to be etched into their awareness.

If Dareen Tatour had lived in a village near Ramallah, I believe nobody would ask her if she's a poet. They would jail her without charges for incitement. But within the Green Line, such measures are extreme, so it must be proved that she isn't a poet. In the end, the prosecutor is doing what she's supposed to do: to frighten, to deter, to censor poetry and to turn a poet into an enemy. All that remains is to call her an "inciter." If we say it enough, it will succeed. And what about all those who weren't suspected of incitement, despite their words. A senior MK ("Anyone who pulls out a knife or a screwdriver — you have to shoot him to kill"); a senior Likud member ("The Sudanese are a cancer in our body") and a prime minister ("The Arab voters are going in droves to the polls"). The list goes on.

Nobody in the courtroom could see that this was a theater of the absurd: That before us was a prosecutor arguing in Hebrew about the interpretation of Arabic words, whose meaning can be understood only within the Arabic poetic tradition. Whereas the debate was not about the poem, or about its quality, but about the quality of the translation into Hebrew.

And still, within all this confusion, with the learned assistance of the prosecutor we learned several basic facts about the state of culture in Israel. What is a poem in Arabic: One that can be explained in Hebrew, because in the original language it has no existence. What is a translation: That which uproots the sapling from its soil and its cultural environment and plants it in foreign soil in order to create a Tower of Babel of words. Who is a translator? Some who is authorized by the government to find a for every word in Arabic only one interpretation in Hebrew. What is a prosecution: That which will do anything in its power to prevent Palestinian national poetry within the boundaries of the Green Line. And what is a poet? Someone who reveals the depths of her soul and the lies of the government. The prosecution's question reveal what it is trying to conceal: That there are people who are groaning under oppression and loss of rights and are not eligible for privileges like the Jews.

In a response statement, the State Prosecutor's Office said that every judicial proceeding in Israel is conducted in Hebrew, including the one under discussion. "At the same time, the course of the discussion was translated for the accused into Arabic by a court-appointed interpreter, even though the accused is a Hebrew speaker.

"As far as the content is concerned, as indicated by what is attributed to the accused in the indictment, this is a poem that was publicized as part of a video clip showing violent scenes from the intifada, and not as a separate text.

"The translation of the text that accompanied the video was done by a veteran policeman whose mother tongue is Arabic. It's a literal translation that didn't presume to interpret the words."

First published: https://www.haaretz.com/israel-news/.premium-1.805520

Over 150 writers, poets, translators, editors, artists, public intellectuals, and cutural workers — including Alice Walker, Naomi Klein, and Jacqueline Woodson — have signed a petition urging Tatour's release. The petition, at Jewish Voices for Peace, is still open to signatories.

Submissions to Botsotso magazine & website

All submissions are welcome. Please send original, unpublished work in any South African language and be careful to keep a copy as we cannot be held responsible for loss or damage to manuscripts and cannot return work.

Simultaneous submission of the same work to several magazines/publishers is not acceptable. However, should you wish to withdraw work from Botsotso kindly inform us timeously. All work received is considered by the editorial board but due to the high volume of work received we are not always able to respond to each contributor. As such please bear with us if you do not receive feedback!

No payment for published work is offered as our budget is very limited but selected work will qualify you for a complimentary copy of the magazine. Copyright of all published material remains with the writer/artist but the proceeds from the sale of Botsotso magazine are used for new projects. As a non-profit entity we are struggling to achieve financial self-sufficiency – a very difficult goal to achieve as the "market" for new, original South African writing (especially for poetry and short fiction) is extremely small.

Please remember to include your contact details: name, postal and email address, telephone number.

Botsotso magazine appears irregularly as a number of important variables have to be satisfied – quality and diversity of submissions, funding, time to edit – but we do attempt to produce at least one edition a year. Some work is included in both the electronic and hard copy versions of Botsotso but we reserve the right to publish in one or the other as circumstances change.

Botsotso
Box 30952, Braamfontein, 2017
or
botsotso@artslink.co.za

Printed in the United States
By Bookmasters